The 5th Anniversary Edition

1001

Ways To Be
ROMANTIC®

—∽—

Gregory J.P. Godek

A Handbook for Men

∽

A Godsend to Women

Romance Across America™
1996-'97

Gregory J.P. Godek's 50-State/150-City/21-Month Book Tour

Greg will be bringing his Romance Seminar to all of America in 1996 and 1997. He and his wife, Tracey, will be touring the country in their 36-foot Holiday Rambler RV {"Romance Vehicle"}. They invite you to participate in a seminar, enjoy a once-in-a-lifetime experience, and make an investment in your relationship. For regular updates on the "Romance Across America" tour, send your name and address to: LoveLetter, P.O. Box 226, Weymouth MA 02188. Or call 800-LOVE-026.

Tour highlights

- ∽ The trip will cover all 50 states.
- ∽ Romance Seminars will be held in 150 cities.
- ∽ 96% of the U.S. population will be within 100 miles of Godek's events.
- ∽ Total trip mileage is 21,037 miles.
- ∽ The trip will be conducted over 21 months—
  February 1996 through October 1997.
- ∽ Booksignings will be held in 500 bookstores—
  that's 10% of all the bookstores in America.

⅌

Casablanca Press,™ Inc.
Boston ✦ Sydney

Bookstore distribution: Login Publishers Consortium
800-626-4330

∽

Giftstore distribution: Sourcebooks
800-727-8866

The 5th Anniversary Edition

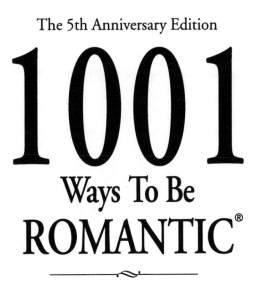

1001
Ways To Be
ROMANTIC®

Gregory J.P. Godek

~

"I like your book '1001 Ways To Be Romantic'! It will fill your brain with all kinds of wonderful romantic ideas. I like number 584!"
~ OPRAH WINFREY

~

"Greg Godek should be nominated for the Nobel Peace Prize for teaching 1001 Ways To Be Romantic."
~ BOSTON MAGAZINE

~

"These books are worth memorizing."
~ BOSTON HERALD

~

"The book is a well-thumbed romantic Bible that I consult often."
~ B. WICKER, READER

~

"Greg's thoughtful, loving books are exciting and intoxicating . . . may we all become blissfully drunk on love."
~ MARK VICTOR HANSEN
CO-AUTHOR OF *CHICKEN SOUP FOR THE SOUL*

~

~

*"1001 Ways To Be Romantic. That seems like an **awful lot.** I mean, guys, if the **first** thousand ideas don't work—what are the chances she's going to stick around when you say, 'Okay, just **one more'?!"***

~ JAY LENO, THE TONIGHT SHOW

~

*"Greg Godek is a **thirty**something Leo Buscaglia."*

~ EVENING MAGAZINE

~

"Godek . . . is helping transform men and women into modern Romeos and Juliets."

~ UPI

~

"Tracey may be married to possibly the most romantic man in the world."

~ WOMAN'S WORLD

~

*"Yes, Greg **does** practice what he preaches."*

~ TRACEY E. GODEK

~

∾

**"1001 Ways To Be Romantic®" is a federally registered trademark of
Casablanca Press™, Inc. and Gregory J.P. Godek,**
denoting a series of products and services including (but certainly not limited to)
books, newsletters, calendars, audio cassette tapes, videotapes, CDs, music collections,
coupons, product kits, gift collections, catalogs, greeting cards, games, doo-dads,
Internet services, speeches, seminars and workshops, documentaries and TV shows—
and anything else we can think of.

The following are trademarks of Casablanca Press & Gregory J.P. Godek:
"LoveStories," "LoveLetter," "Romance 101," "Casablanca Press," "LoveTalks,"
"America's Romance Coach," "America's #1 Romantic," "365 Days of Romance,"
"Changing the world—one couple at a time," "Team Romance USA," "A Little
Romance," "A Little Romance," "The Portable Romantic," "The Lovers' Bedside
Companion," "Romance Across America."

∾

Eighteenth printing. ✦ Printed in the United States of America.
10 9 8 7 6 5 4 3

∾

Published by **Casablanca Press™, Inc.**
P.O. Box 226, Weymouth, Massachusetts 02188-0001 ✦ 617-340-1300

∾

Info Line/Book orders/Seminar dates & tickets ✦ 800-LOVE-026
Visit Greg's Romance Page on the Internet! ✦ http://www.godek.com

∾

Cover rose in *calligraphy* by Maria Thomas at Pendragon, Ink. ✦ 508-234-6843
Cover design by Mary-Lynne Bohn ✦ 508-287-1448
Book design by Bruce Jones Design, Inc. ✦ 617-350-6160
Media relations/PR and stuff by Cone Communications ✦ 617-227-2111

∾

Publisher's Cataloging in Publication Data
Godek, Gregory J.P., 1955-
1001 Ways To Be Romantic
Includes index.
1. Relationships. 2. Psychology. 3. Self-help. 4. How-to. I. Title.
Library of Congress Catalog Card Number: 91-92117

∾

ISBN 0-883518-05-9

Dedications

This book is dedicated to the thousands of women
who asked that it be written . . . and to the millions of men
who desperately need it.

And, of course, to my Bride . . .
I.L.Y.—A.D.Y.F.I. (F.A.S!)
L.B.I.T.

✦ **Contents** ✦

1001 Ways To Be Romantic—

✦ Contents ✦

—*Organized into 100 chapters*

Acknowledgments

Tracey
Bruce
Courtney
Gerald Rosenthal
Kate Broughton
Betsy Seeley
Boston Center for Adult Education
The Main Course
Mary Ann Sabia
Andy Pallotta
Mary-Lynne Bohn
Mj
John & Jean
Warren & Judy
Maria Thomas & Pendragon, Ink.
Dominique & Mitch & Ben & Pat
Wayne Johnson
John "JB" Bentz
Publishers Marketing Association
National Speakers Association
Bill McHugh & Kim Molloy & Courier Corp.
Patricia Wiklund
Nancy Michaels
Steven Jobs
H.S.
Lou Rizzo & UPS
Sam & The Group
Kate & Tom & Colleen (& Jake & Duffy)
Dr. Augustus & Maria Falcone
Orin & DaBen
Paul Ferrini
Richard Price & Graphic Illusions
Candy Means
Timothy Corbett
Brit
Wolfgang Amadeus Mozart

About the Author

Gregory J.P. Godek is a writer, professional speaker, newlywed and incurable romantic. He was romantic by inclination long before it became an avocation, then preoccupation—and finally—occupation. Greg has been researching relationships and teaching his acclaimed Romance Seminar for more than 15 years. ∼ This book was written at the request of thousands of women. ∼ Greg once said that the world doesn't need yet another advice book offering the latest psychological cure-all. We also don't need another "cute" book on *Love* (which men would never read, anyway). What people *do* need—and keep asking for—is a return to the basics: In this case, Good Old-Fashioned Romance (with appropriate updates for the modern world). What people need is a *practical* book filled with *specific* ideas—because they don't need to be coddled, they need a handy reference and (occasionally) a good swift kick-in-the-pants. This book is both. ∼ Greg's also said that this book *could* be called "My World And Welcome To It" (with a friendly nod to James Thurber)—because it's *really* a book about himself: His view of life, his personal philosophy, his love for women (one in particular, and all of them in general), his observations about relationships, and his mighty collection of articles, resources, references, personal notes and comics. ∼ This book is for everyone who wants to bring more joy, happiness, peace, fun and passion into their lives. Greg isn't so bold as to believe that romance is THE answer, but suggests that it is ONE of the answers. It is his Way.

∞

Since the first edition of this book was published five years ago, Greg has: Taught romance on *Oprah;* sold 1 million books; discussed "Is Your Lover 'Romantically Impaired?' on *Donahue;* taught romance to the U.S. Army; written five *more* books; been published in five foreign countries; and planned the biggest book tour in history—the 50-state/150-city/ 21-month "Romance Across America" tour. ∼ Greg is a rarity— A celebrity who actually practices what he preaches: He really *does* have a happy marriage. For Greg, romance isn't about academic theories, trendy concepts or advice dispensed from On High. It is about *life*—living it well, experiencing it fully, and sharing it lovingly.

Author's Note

Welcome to the **5th Anniversary Edition of** *1001 Ways To Be Romantic.*
You are entering a world of romantic love, inspired fun, renewed hope and
creative expression.

❖ To new readers—a warm *Hello.*
❖ To old friends—*Welcome back!*

This edition is expanded, revised, and 64 pages longer than the earlier
editions of the book. It includes a new section of LoveStories—true and
inspiring stories from regular people; plus a bonus section with an *additional*
101 ways to be romantic. The publisher wanted me to save them for a
future book, but I insisted on sharing them with you *now.* ∼ I extend a
personal invitation to all of you to participate in one of my Romance
Seminars as I travel through all 50 states during 1996 and 1997 in the
"Romance Across America" tour. (See page 323 for more info.) ∼ Thanks
for picking-up *1001 Ways To Be Romantic.* If you enjoy reading it *half* as
much as I enjoyed writing it, I'll consider myself quite lucky. And if you
enjoy *living* it half as much as *I* enjoy living it, then I . . . well, I think I will
have fulfilled some kind of Higher Purpose. Your suggestions and ideas for
future books and *The LoveLetter Newsletter* are most welcome!

NAMASTE, GREGORY J.P. GODEK
21 AUGUST 1995

Publisher's Note

Every effort has been made to ensure the accuracy of information in this
book. Errors will be gratefully corrected in the next printing. To express our
gratitude, we'll send you a free copy of *The Lovers' Bedside Companion,* if
you'll send us any corrections. Really! ∼ Please note: Punctuation and
odd word choice are off-limits, since Mr. Godek insists on bending the Basic
Rules of Grammar and Usage to his own artistic purposes. Our apologies to
language purists, William Safire, and English teachers everywhere.

Foreword

By Mark Victor Hansen
Co-author of the New York Times Best-selling series
Chicken Soup for the Soul

Greg Godek personifies the love that he so eloquently and persuasively writes about in *1001 Ways To Be Romantic*. He loves himself positively and correctly. His healthy self-love and self-esteem allow him to pour deep and profound love into his writings. He so thoroughly believes in his work that after publication he enthusiastically spreads the word to attract the widest possible readership. He sells *millions* of books, helping millions of us to better understand our most important value—LOVE. ∼ Helping millions of readers to embrace love and live in an exhalted state of love makes the world an infinitely better place in which to live, thrive, move and have our being. I'll just bet that if Greg could, he would have *everyone* read, understand and act on his reflections on the enchanted state of love. ∼ If that were to happen, we could cease war because individuals like Hitler and Sadam Hussein, who were abused early in their lives and lack love, create war. Hussein's internalized assumption is that if he had enough power and control over enough people, he would be *loved*. Nothing could be further from the truth. ∼ Greg teaches the truth. The truth is that love comes from the inside-out, not the outside-in. When we have internalized enough self-worth, self-acceptance and self-love we create the mirror equivalent of that in our outside world. ∼ Greg's throughtful, loving books are exciting and intoxicating . . . may we all become blissfully drunk on love.

MARK VICTOR HANSEN
KONA, HAWAII
AUGUST 1995

Books by Gregory J.P. Godek

1001 Ways To Be Romantic
1001 More Ways To Be Romantic
Romance 101
The Portable Romantic
The Lovers' Bedside Companion
Loving: A Journal of Our Relationship

The 5th Anniversary Edition

1001

Ways To Be
ROMANTIC®

Romance 101

1

Romance is a state of mind. If you have the right mindset, you can make cleaning the bathroom romantic; if you have the *wrong* mindset, you can turn a moonlit stroll on the beach into a fight.

2

Romance is about the little things. It's much more about the small gestures— the little ways of making daily life with your lover a bit more special—than it is about extravagant, expensive gestures. (Although the outrageous certainly has its place in the romantic's repertoire.)

3

There are *two* kinds of romance:

1) **Obligatory romance**
2) **Optional romance**

Both are important, and although my focus is on *optional* romance, beginners are advised to be careful not to overlook the obligatory. But make no mistake about it: *Optional romance is more genuinely romantic.*

➤ **Obligatory romance** includes: Celebrating her birthday; getting him a gift for Christmas/the Holiday Season; acknowledging your anniversary; remembering Valentine's Day.

➤ **Optional romance** includes: *Everything else.* Little surprises. Big surprises. Candlelit dinners. Champagne toasts. Weekend get-aways. Sending funny greeting cards, romantic cards, sexy cards, home-made cards. Escaping from the kids. Exercising your creativity. Massages. Surprise "dates" in the middle of the week. Romantic movies. Love letters.

4

Why be romantic? Why bother? Simple . . .
It will improve the quality of your life.

5

Romance is not gender-specific. Nearly every idea in this book applies to *both* men and women, even though I sometimes say "her" and other times "his." Don't forget that deep down, we all want the same things in life. Men and women have different *styles*—not different needs.

When I started teaching the Romance Class 15 years ago, it was sub-titled "For Men Only," which seemed perfectly appropriate to me . . . because let's face it, most guys need a good swift kick when it comes to romance. After about a year, women began asking why they were being excluded. I realized that there *wasn't* any reason, so I expanded the class to include them. The combination of men and women together was great! The sharing, the give-and-take, and the opportunity for couples to attend together, all combined to make the class especially successful for participants.

6

Listen! With your ears, mind and heart. Listen for the meaning behind his actions. Listen for the message behind her words.

7

Being romantic *occasionally* is one thing, but *living a romantic life requires consistency of effort.* Making romantic gestures is watering the flower of your relationship. Don't let it wilt!

8

Overdo something. Does he love **m**&**m**'s? Buy him 50 pounds!!

9

Give your partner choices. Fast or slow? Gold or silver? Now or later? Large or small? Today or tomorrow? Red or blue? Classic or avant-garde? Conservative or outrageous? Public or private? Expensive or not? Modern or antique? Here or there?

10-11

✦ "Tune-in" to romantic opportunities. They're all around you! On TV. On the radio. In newspapers and magazines. In shop windows.

✦ Start with the basics, then *give 'em a twist!* Your own creativity is your greatest romantic resource.

12

Romance is the expression of love. It's not the *same* as love, but it's the *language of love.*

10 Tips That Will Change Your Life

13

Turn the ordinary into the special.

You can turn everyday events into "little celebrations"—opportunities to express your love for your partner. We're not talking *passion* here, but *affection*. [We'll get to passion elsewhere . . .] A tiny bit of forethought can turn the ordinary into the special. Eat dinner by candlelight. Tie a ribbon around a cup of bedtime tea. Pop your own popcorn while watching a video at home. Turn his birth*day* into a birthday *month!* Give her a bottle of champagne as a "thank you" for doing the grocery shopping. Leave a greeting card on his car seat when he's about to run errands for you.

14

Recognize that one mode of expression isn't enough!

Love can be—and should be—expressed in *many* ways. But most of us settle into one mode that's comfortable for us. And while it's familiar to you, it becomes *boring* for your partner.

➤ Some of you are *verbal.* You share your feelings with your husband a lot. That's great. But you've got to back it up with some modes of expression that communicate caring on other levels, too. Do you share his interest in football, cars, bird-watching? Do you occasionally dress in his favorite outfit?

➤ Some of you are *action-oriented.* You "prove" your love for your wife by "bringing home the bacon," and taking out the garbage. That's all well and good, but you've got to bring her flowers occasionally, and call her from the office just to say "I love you."

15

Recapture the fun in your relationship by viewing romance as "Adult Play."

Some people—especially men—tend to view romance as a serious (somber!) and difficult activity. Nothing could be further from the truth! True romance is *easy* because it's simply an expression of what's already inside you: Your feelings of love, caring and passion for your partner.

> **"We don't stop playing because we grow old;**
> **we grow old because we stop playing."**
>
> ~ GEORGE BERNARD SHAW

The concept of *adult play* is a reminder to loosen up, be creative, and remember the fun and passion you had early in your relationship. Adults need to *re-learn* how to play—something that came naturally to all of us as children. Many ideas in this book are essentially exercises in playing.

16

*Understand the difference between a **gift** and a **present**.*

❦ A *present* is something you're giving the receiver because it's something **you** *want him or her to have.*

❦ A *gift* is something that you're sure *the **receiver** wants.*

When a man gives a woman lingerie, nine times out of ten it's a *present*. When he gives her favorite perfume, it's a *gift*. This is not to say that one is better than the other. Gifts and presents are just *different*. Knowing the difference between a gift and a present will help both of you stay "in-tune" with each other and avoid unrealistic expectations and possible hard feelings.

☞ Note #1: Items can sometimes be both gifts and presents at the same time.

☞ Note #2: Because the words *gift* and *present* are commonly used as synonyms, I will use them interchangeably in the remainder of the book for the sake of simplicity.

17

Romance is a balance of two concepts:

1) **Actions speak louder than words.**
2) **It's the thought that counts.**

These concepts are two sides of the same coin. Think about it.

Romance is the process. Love is the goal.

~ GJPG

18

Let other things speak for you.

You don't have to be eloquent in order to be romantic. You don't have to write great poetry or even mediocre love letters.

★ Let these people speak for you: William Shakespeare, Billy Joel, Paul McCartney, Charlie Brown, Susan Polis Schutz, Elizabeth Barrett Browning, Kahlil Gibran.

★ Let these *things* speak for you: Flowers, stuffed animals, greeting cards, songs, comic strips, newspaper headlines.

19

Romance is the icing on the cake.

Romance makes your relationship sweeter, more fun, more elegant—but it's not the cake. Your *relationship* is the cake.

20

Try to overcome The Romantic Law of Inverse Proportions:

❤ The more you need romance in your life, the less likely you are to do it; the less you need it, the more likely you are to do it.

Admittedly, some of us overdo it. [You'd have to be a fanatic to write this book, right?! It's just so much fun that it's hard to slow down.]

However, most people need *more* romance in their lives, but they're too preoccupied with other things to even recognize the lack.

❤ There's a very simple test to determine if you're romantic enough: Simply ask your partner. His or her answer is the truth, whether you want to accept it or not.

21

Pay attention to the "Afterglow Effect."

After you've made a romantic gesture, there's a certain "afterglow" that lingers. Your partner appreciates you more, is nicer to you, and is likely to respond in kind. You feel more loved, and bask in the glow of having given something special to your lover.

Romance is not an end unto itself. It's about enjoying your life more fully—living passionately in partnership with your lover. The most successful relationships seem to be surrounded by a perpetual "afterglow." Several older couples in the Romance Class seem to radiate a special warmth. When asked what their secret of long-term marital happiness is, they tend to describe a kind of "quiet romance."

22

Remember: Romance isn't barter!

You'll lose every time if you use romantic gestures to barter for favors or forgiveness. The following "unspoken agreements" may have had some validity in the past, but in the 1990s they don't cut it anymore:

✦ I'll take you to a movie and dinner if you'll sleep with me.
✦ I'll cook dinner for you if you'll let me nag you.
✦ I'll give you flowers if you'll forgive me for being a jerk.

Romance is the expression of your love for that special person. It's not a bargaining chip. When you use it as one, you cheapen the gesture, devalue your relationship, and up the ante for the next round of bartering.

Classic Romance

23

Make a toast to one another every time you hold a wine glass. Make eye contact. Take turns making the toast. Whisper it.

24

Revive chivalry. Women love a real Gentleman.

➳ Open her car door. Hold her dinner chair. Help her on with her coat.
➳ Older women will love the revival of manners.
➳ Younger women will need to be re-trained to see these gestures as tokens of respect and affection, and not as messages that men feel women are inferior and helpless.

25

Go out dancing! Ballroom dancing is enjoying a resurgence unlike anything since WW II. Glenn Miller, Benny Goodman and the Big Band sound are once again being heard in dance halls, restaurants, clubs and church basements throughout the land.

26

What could be more classic than a fine gold locket with your photo inside?

27

Serenade her. Sing her favorite love song, or "your song" to her. You don't need to have a great voice. Your sincerity will more than make up for your lack of perfect pitch.

★ Get a good friend to accompany you on guitar.

★ See the chapter called "Making Beautiful Music Together" to learn about a great device that will eliminate the lead singer's voice from any recorded song—enabling you to sing the lead, with the same back-up from the original recording!

★ If you have a truly atrocious voice, hire a singer/guitar player to serenade her. For a more personal touch, have him sing a song that *you* wrote.

28

A true classic is the lazy-Sunday-afternoon-canoe-ride on a calm, beautiful pond. Dress in your Sunday best, pack a picnic lunch, and enjoy!

29

Write him a love letter! ✳ Pen her a poem! ✳ Compose him a song!

Be Prepared!

30

Be prepared for spontaneous romantic escapes! Have "His" and "Hers" overnight bags packed at all times. Keep under the bed or in the car trunk.

31

Go out this weekend and buy $50 worth of greeting cards. Don't ask questions, *just do it!* Head for your nearest card shop and spend a solid hour. reading hundreds of cards. Read all the Far Side cards! Scan all the Peanuts cards. Find the sexy cards. Get *several* birthday cards. Choose piles of friendship cards. Get some sentimental ones. Don't forget cards with no inscription, so you can exercise your creativity.

Now you'll be prepared for anything!

❦ Don't forget to file some of these cards at work.
❦ Pre-stamp the envelopes (with *Love Stamps*) to save time later.

32

Be prepared for shopping! Know *all* of your partner's sizes! You should be able to buy *any* item of clothing for him or her, and have it fit 80% of the time.

☞ Could you buy her *any* item of lingerie? A coat? A sweater?
☞ Could you buy him a pair of shoes? A pair of gloves? A *hat?*

33

Be prepared with a romantic music library. (See these chapters for specific musical suggestions: "Lovesongs" and "Making Beautiful Music Together.")

34

Be prepared to create the proper ambiance for romance. Not only do you need great romantic background music, you need a way to *play it non-stop for several hours.* Get a tape player with auto-reverse; or get a CD player with slots for three or more discs. Nothing breaks the mood like getting up in the middle of a romantic dinner, intimate discussion or lovemaking session, to turn over the darn record!

35

Be prepared to move straight into cuddling and sleeping after lovemaking . . . If you wear contact lenses, trade your regular lenses for *extended wear* lenses. Why? So you won't have to break the mood after lovemaking to get up and wash, rinse and disinfect those lenses! Those of us without 20/20 vision don't particularly like our other options: Either wearing glasses to bed, or seeing everything in a blur.

❧♪❧♪❧♪❧♪❧♪❧♪❧♪❧♪❧♪❧♪❧♪❧

Romance is about the little things.

~ GJPG

❧♪❧♪❧♪❧♪❧♪❧♪❧♪❧♪❧♪❧♪❧♪❧

36

Mark all significant dates in your appointment or business calendar. (Birthdays, anniversaries, Valentine's Day, and other personally-significant days . . .) Then, write-in reminders to send cards or buy gifts *at least one week in advance of the upcoming date!*

37

Another way to ensure that you get those greeting cards, notes and gifts out on time is to get a 3-ring binder with 12 dividers with pockets. Label them with the months, and insert relevant items into each pocket. Attach a "Master List" of significant dates to the inside cover. This way, you'll usually be prepared well in advance of every event that comes along.

✔ Insert greeting cards, notes, poems, articles, reminders to yourself, ads, catalog pages, etc.

✔ Make sure *every* pocket has stuff in it—especially for those months that include no "official" anniversaries or holidays. Make up your own holidays and reasons for celebrating!

38

Make a list of at least 10 things you *know* she'd love. Don't put this off till later—*do it right now!*

39-46

Be prepared—for anything! Always have on hand:

❦ A bottle of champagne
❦ Love Stamps
❦ A few candles
❦ A fun, silly and/or cheap "Trinket Gift"

❦ A serious/romantic greeting card
❦ A funny/romantic greeting card
❦ A nice lingerie gift
❦ An album or CD of special romantic music

47

Write "Romantic Reminders" on your "To Do" list at work. (What's the use of being a great success in the business world if you're a miserable failure in your personal life?) Romantic Reminders will remind you that there's another part of your life that's quite important.

48

Create a "Gift Closet." Get gifts ahead of time; buy things on sale; order quantities of items and get discounts; buy things during end-of-season sales; pick up presents on a whim. Then warehouse them and save them for later!

✦ Never again will you have to rush around at the last minute looking for an anniversary gift.
✦ You'll have more fun giving gifts and presents.
✦ Your partner will appreciate it.
✦ You'll save money!
✦ You'll be prepared to surprise her whenever the inspiration strikes you.
✦ If you live in a very small house or apartment, create a "Gift Drawer" or store a "Gift Box" under your bed.

49

Be prepared to giftwrap your gifts. (Reminder for guys especially: The presentation is nearly as important as the gift itself.) Thus, have extra wrapping paper, bows, ribbon and boxes around at all times.

50

(For those of you with two left thumbs . . .) Be prepared—for instant, hassle-free giftwrapping. Buy fancy bags and pre-decorated boxes for packaging up those quickie gifts.

51

Carry stamps in your wallet at all times! (Preferably several *Love Stamps!*)

52

A great way to "be prepared" is to team-up with a good, local travel agent. Become a regular customer and you'll get preferential treatment and early notification of special travel deals on the horizon.

Be Creative!

53

Make your own greeting cards. Store-bought cards are fine—I have a drawer full of them . . . but home-made cards are extra special. You don't have to be artistic, just heartfelt. (Remember, she's with you not because you're Picasso, but because you're *you.*)

54

Make a "Commemorative Scroll" to celebrate his birthday, your anniversary, or any special year.

☞ Pick the year.

☞ Research the major happenings of that year.

　　✳ Here are some suggested categories:
　　　In the News, Advertising, TV, Radio, Quotable Quotes, Movies, Broadway, Music, Sports, Art, Books, Fashion, Scientific Breakthroughs, Politics, World Events, Religion, Daily Life, Miscellany.

☞ See #756 for two invaluable books that provide all the information you'll need for this little project.

☞ Write-it-up, type-it-up, word-process-it or calligraphy-it. Present it!

55

Hiding places for notes and small gifts:

* ✫ Under the pillow
* ✫ In the glove compartment
* ✫ In the medicine cabinet
* ✫ In the refrigerator
* ✫ In his briefcase
* ✫ In her purse
* ✫ In a pizza box
* ✫ Under his dinner plate

56

Truly mischievous romantics go to great lengths to hide gifts and notes. Herewith are some suggestions from the more off-the-wall students of the Romance Class:

* ✫ Carefully open various product packages, insert the item, and carefully re-seal the package. Favorite targets include cereal boxes, soup cans, ice cream cartons, bags of m&m's, candy bars, soda cans, and, of course, boxes of Cracker Jacks!
* ✫ Notes have appeared frozen in ice cubes, floating in punch bowls, hidden among bouquets and tied to balloons.

57

Want some suggestions for notes, gifts and trinkets to hide? Again, from Romance Class participants:

* ✦ Friendship rings
* ✦ Earrings
* ✦ Condoms
* ✦ Far Side comics
* ✦ Hockey tickets
* ✦ Love Coupons
* ✦ Invitations to dinner
* ✦ Invitations to sex
* ✦ Theatre tickets
* ✦ Valentine conversation hearts

58

Is she a crossword fanatic? Create a custom crossword puzzle. Make the clues reminiscent of your relationship and life together; include private jokes, funny phrases and names of favorite songs.

59

Make him *work* for his next gift! Leave written clues that lead him on a wild goose chase around the house, through the yard, to the neighbors or around town.

60

Make a "Mission Impossible" tape.

❋ "Your assignment, should you choose to accept it . . . is to meet a hand-some, dark-haired stranger for a romantic dinner at the Posh Cafe, to-morrow evening at 7:00 p.m. I suggest you take on the role of a myste-rious and ravishing beauty . . . "

❋ Leave the cassette tape in a Walkman with a note, "Play me."

If your relationship were a painting, what would it look like?

~ GJPG

61-64

Create "theme" gifts and presentations. Combine similar items and ideas to create fun, meaningful gifts.

❦ Give her these two gifts, wrapped separately but ribboned together:
   ☆ The poetry book *A Friend Forever*, by Susan Polis Schutz
   ☆ The album *Forever Friends*, by Justo Almario

❦ Give him *all* of Leo Buscaglia's "love" books . . .
   ★ *Love*
   ★ *Personhood*
   ★ *Living Loving & Learning*

   . . . and/or get some of Leo's great talks on videotape.

❦ Give her a new pair of comfortable walking shoes or hiking boots plus a copy of the book *Off The Beaten Path—A guide to more than 1,000 scenic and interesting places still uncrowded and inviting.* (If you wanted to continue the theme to another level, you could arrange a vacation to one of these spots.)

❦ Does he *love* Beethoven? Get him recordings of all 9 symphonies, along with 9 red roses, 9 balloons and 9 little love notes.

   ☆ If it's Mozart he loves, you'll have to buy 42 symphonies.

   ☆ And if it's Haydn he loves, you're *really* in trouble, because Papa Haydn composed an incredible 108 symphonies!

65

Create a "Romantic Idea Jar."

✦ Write 100 romantic ideas on separate slips of paper. Fill a jar with them. Once a week, one of you picks an idea at random, and has to implement it within the next week. Take turns being the chooser every other week.

✦ Or, number slips of paper 1 through 1001. Pick a number, then refer to the corresponding number in this book. (For this activity, you may want to skip the numbers in the chapter "Spare No Expense"!)

Flowers

66

You may forget your Social Security number, your e-mail address, or your anniversary (although I *hope* not!)—but here's one important number that you should never forget:18003569377. But wait—here's an easier way to remember it:

1-800-FLOWERS

It's like having a local flower shop at your fingertips 24 hours a day, 7 days a week! The freshest flowers, unique and exciting arrangements, on-time delivery, expert floral advice and friendly service. What more could you ask for?!

67

When traveling, give her a rose for each day you'll be away.

68

Scientific surveys reveal that 99% of all women *love* flowers. (The other 1% fall into the Practical/Logical minority: They'd rather have the *cash*.)

Flowers are great not only because they're appreciated, but because they're easy to order by phone; because flower shops grow conveniently on every corner; and because flowers come in every price range.

- ❀ Bring home a bouquet.
- ❀ Give her one red rose.
- ❀ Select her favorite flower.

69

The Perpetual Bouquet™. Bring home one flower a day for a week or two or three. You'll create a wonderfully diverse bouquet day-by-day. It gives both of you something to look forward to, and you'll have an ever-changing, always-fresh reminder of your love.

70

(Men like flowers, too.)

71

Place a flower under the windshield wiper of his car.

❀❀❀❀❀❀❀❀❀❀❀❀

Romance is the language of love.

~ GJPG

❀❀❀❀❀❀❀❀❀❀❀❀

72

Get to know your local florist. Become a "regular"—you'll get better service and fresher flowers!

73

Speaking of fresh flowers . . . always ask *specifically* for fresh flowers. A good, fresh rose should last nearly a week, while an older one can wilt in less than a day. (Tip from a reader: A solution of one part 7-Up to 2 parts water is great for keeping cut flowers fresher longer.)

74

Buy her a beautiful crystal vase (or a bud vase, if you're on a budget). Not only does it make a great gift, but it will encourage both of you to brighten up your lives with flowers more often.

75

"Flying flowers" is what some enthusiasts call butterflies. Visit a "butterfly aviary" for an enchanting experience!

- ✿ *Butterfly World,* Coconut Creek, Florida: 305-977-4400
- ✿ *San Diego Wild Animal Park* (The "Hidden Jungle"): 619-747-8702
- ✿ *Butterfly Place,* Westford, Massachusetts: 508-392-0955
- ✿ *Fort Wayne Children's Zoo,* Indiana: 219-482-4610

76

Use a flower as a "private signal." One couple in the Romance Class told us that for years they've used the "Flower-on-the-Pillow" as a signal that they're interested in making love that night. Sounds good to me!

77

Place a flower in his briefcase.

78

Pick a ❀ daisy. Attach a note to it that ❀ says "She loves me—she loves me not . . . " (For those of you who ❀ don't like to take chances, count the number of ❀ petals first, and do any necessary ❀ pruning!)

79

Did you know . . . that different colored roses have different meanings?

- Red = *PASSION!*
- Pink = friendship
- Yellow = R E S P E C T
- White = PURITY

You singles should pay special attention to this. Early in a relationship is often too soon to send red roses. Send pink or yellow. (Women notice these things.)

80

- Give him one sunflower. Attach a note: "You are the sunshine of my life. (With love from me and Stevie Wonder!)"
- Give her tulips. Attach a note: "I've got two-lips waiting for you!"
- Give her forget-me-nots: Attach a note: "Forget-me-not. I love you."

81

✦ What's in a name?

Rose	Daisy	Lily
Ivy	Black-eyed Susan	Iris

✦ How about *nicknames!?*

Buttercup	Poppy	Sweet Pea

82

Place a flower on her pillow. Just because.

83

Send *one rose.* The power of simplicity. (The note: "This bud's for you!")

84

Your favorite flowers aren't necessarily the most *fragrant* ones. Create a bouquet of especially fragrant flowers, and your romantic gesture will take on a whole new dimension: You'll fill the entire house with an aromatic reminder of your love.

Ask for:

* ❀ Freesia
* ❀ Rubrum lilies
* ❀ Lilacs
* ❀ Roses
* ❀ Stock
* ❀ Gardenias
* ❀ Casablanca lilies
* ❀ Stephanotis

85

A rose is a rose is a rose—right? Well, it seems that not all roses were created equal. The *Prelude* Rose is a medium-sized mauve/lilac rose known for its especially strong fragrance. It was introduced in the U.S. in 1990. Ask for it . . . or for its cousin, the *Preview* Rose—a similarly fragrant *white* rose.

All I really need is love, but a little chocolate now and then doesn't hurt!

~ LUCY VAN PELT
IN PEANUTS, BY CHARLES M. SCHULZ

Chocolate

86

Chocolate! There's just something about it, isn't there?! While I firmly believe that romance shouldn't be used as a bribe to curry favors, a box of great chocolates is an incredibly well-received gift, isn't it?

87

800-9GODIVA

88

Reliable sources report that chocolate may *just really be* an aphrodisiac.

☐ **Fact:** Chocolate contains large amounts of phenylethylamine, a chemical that is also naturally produced by the body when one has feelings of love.

☐ **Observation:** 99% of all women love chocolate. 50% of them *really* love chocolate. 25% of them *really, really* love chocolate. And 2% of them *really, really, really* love chocolate!

☐ **Fact:** The Aztecs considered chocolate to be so powerful a stimulant that women were forbidden from having it!

89

A lifelong passion for chocolate inspired one couple in the Romance Class to embark on a round-the-world search for the Ultimate Chocolate. They actually arrange their vacations so they can visit all of the major chocolate manufacturers in various countries! (You might consider your own, scaled-down search—with taste-testing sessions, comparing Hershey's with Nestle's with Godiva with Fanny Farmer with Whitman's!)

90-93

Here are some reports and travel suggestions from our fanatical couple:

- Are Swiss chocolates the best in the world? To find out, visit the Nestle chocolate factory in Broc. Write or call for reservations: Nestle S.A., Service des Visites, 1636 Broc FR, Switzerland; (41) 296-5151.
- Chocolat Alprose, located in the Ticino, Switzerland, also offers tasty tours. For reservations: Chocolat Alprose, Via Rompada, 6987 Caselano, Switzerland; (91) 71-6666.
- "The Swiss Plan" is an organization that will arrange package tours to *several* Swiss chocolate factories. Call them at 800-777-9480.
- The "Cadbury World Chocolate Experience" is in Birmingham, England. Cadbury has an exhibit on the *history* of chocolate (which features a taste of a chocolate drink made from an ancient Aztec recipe).

94

ENGLISH

"Excuse me, where is the nearest chocolate?"

FRENCH

"Excusez-moi, où est le chocolat le plus proche?"

GERMAN

"Entschuldigen Sie bitte, wo ist die nächste Schokolade?"

From *Chocolate: The Consuming Passion*, by Sandra Boynton!

95

And closer to home . . . in Hershey, Pennsylvania, is "Chocolate World." After the 15-minute tour of the Hershey chocolate factory you can enjoy the on-site garden, wildlife park and amusement park. For more information call 717-534-4900.

96

Long-stem chocolate roses! Call Lila's Chocolates at 415-383-8887. Only $39 per dozen, delivered to your sweetie's doorstep!

97

"The Embrace," "The Nightcap," and *"The Crush"* are the names of some wild new chocolate creations from Sincerely Gourmet Chocolates. I've yet to discover a chocolate maker that strives to capture the essence of romance as completely or as passionately as these folks! If you're looking for excellent chocolate [perhaps an alternative to Godiva!?] that's elegantly packaged, look no further! Actually, look in upscale department stores and specialty shops! Or call Sincerely Gourmet Chocolates directly, at 800-454-3856 or 305-351-2156. Or write to 4901 Northwest 17th Way, Suite 403, Fort Lauderdale, Florida 33309.

A Touch of Class

98

"Casual yet elegant" describes Shakespeare-In-The-Park, held every summer in New York's Central Park at the Public Theatre. Call the New York Shakespeare Festival at 212-260-2400.

99

Hire a pianist to play during dinner at home.

100

Have his portrait painted from a photograph.

101

Propose a toast to her while at a dinner party with good friends.

102

Make a donation to her favorite charity—instead of going on your next expensive date. You can show her that you care about *her*, and at the same time show you care about the whales or the environment or her favorite cause.

103

When's the last time you visited your local art gallery? Museum? Public garden? Planetarium?

104

When's the last time you attended the symphony? The ballet? The opera? A jazz concert?

How do I love thee? Let me count the ways.

~ ELIZABETH BARRETT BROWNING (SEE #440)

105

You *do* have an elegant fountain pen with which to write love notes and love letters, don't you?! A Mont Blanc pen will add an unparalleled touch of class to your act.

106

Copy a romantic poem—or the words to a great lovesong—onto fancy parchment paper. Frame it.

☞ Then giftwrap it and give it to her.
☞ Or hang it on the wall and wait for her to notice it.

107

Hire a limousine for an elegant evening out.

108

Bring home a bottle of Dom Perignon champagne. Celebrate tonight, or save it for a special occasion. (Just having a bottle of it around adds a touch of class to your house.)

Grow old along with me! The best is yet to be.

~ ROBERT BROWNING

109

Wear a tuxedo home from work. [Women *love* men in tuxes.]

A Change of Pace

110

Eat dinner by candlelight. Heck—eat *breakfast* by candlelight!

111

If you live in the city, take a drive in the country. If you live in the country, visit the nearest city. If you're landlocked, visit the coast. If you're coastal, find a mountain to hike.

112

Shower together. My ongoing poll of Romance Class participants indicates a drastic drop in co-ed showering following the sixth month of serious dating, or fourth month of marriage—whichever comes first. Showering together is not only romantic, it's ecologically responsible.

❦ You can buy *shower heads built-for-two!* They have two nozzles, so one of you doesn't have to shiver while the other showers!

113

Take the "spinner" from an old board game. Draw a new circle and label it with a dozen romantic activities. Tape the spinner to your refrigerator, and take turns giving it a spin once a week! (Re-draw the circle with *new* romantic ideas every few months.)

114

Send a taxi to pick him up after work; pre-pay the cab fare (including tip!), and instruct the driver to take him to your favorite restaurant, where you'll be waiting for him!

115

Trade homes or apartments with a friend for the weekend. It won't cost you a dime, and the change of environment will help refresh you both. It's like taking a mini-vacation close to home.

116

If you have a bit of a weekly budget for romance, you can upgrade the previous concept and stay at a local hotel, taking advantage of the many "Weekend Packages" available. Check-out the major hotel chains—Hilton, Hyatt, Loews, Marriott, Sheraton, Westin—as they all have great "Escape Weekends" or "Romance Weekends"; they also have toll-free numbers for your convenience.

∞∞∞∞∞∞∞∞∞∞∞

When I give my heart away,
You know that it's forever;
As I give my love I give my Word to you.
And as our lives unfold for us,
We'll watch them bloom together,
Every moment we shall see the world anew.

~ Brit Lay, "Wedding Song" (See #439)

∞∞∞∞∞∞∞∞∞∞∞

A Month of Romance

117-144

——— Week 1 ———

Sunday

Buy a guide book for the city or region where you live. Visit someplace you've never been before.

Monday

Check the morning newspaper for his horoscope. Cut it out, write a comment in the margin. Tape it to the bathroom mirror. Or put it in his briefcase. Or stick it in his appointment calendar. Or put it in his pants pocket.

Tuesday

After you say good-bye, turn back one more time and blow her a kiss.

✦ Several couples I know have turned this little routine into a sometimes-funny, sometimes-touching ritual.

✦ One pair even acts out the acceptance of the kiss with the receiver pretending to be smacked on the cheek with the flying kiss! (This idea is especially attractive to mimes and would-be actors.)

Wednesday

Buy a lottery ticket. Give it to her with a note attached:

☆ "Take a chance on me. Your chances are better than one in a million!"
☆ "I hit the jackpot when I married you!"

Thursday

Thursday is gift day! Bring home a bottle of scented massage oil. You figure out the rest . . .

Friday

Plan your weekend together! Figure out how to get those chores done quickly and efficiently, so you'll have time to *be together.*

Saturday

Touch more. Hold hands. Brush her cheek with your lips. Stroke his arm. Rub her neck. Massage his feet. Hug! Kiss her nose. Cuddle! Nibble his ear. Massage her back. Sit on his lap.

Week 2

Sunday

Go for a walk.

* Directions: Find the nearest beach, forest or park.
* Instructions: Stand side-by-side. Hold hands. Walk. Talk.

Monday

Get up with the sun. Enjoy the morning for a change, instead of rushing through your shower, grabbing your coffee and dashing out the door. Have a leisurely breakfast; talk with your partner about your hopes and dreams for the future.

Tuesday

Get up with the sun. Make love. Go to work.

Wednesday

Sign-up for a dance class. Or a cooking class. Or a wine tasting class. Or a massage class. Or a music appreciation class. Or a woodworking class. Or a writing class. Or a drawing class . . .

Thursday

Thursday is gift day! Bring home a bouquet of flowers.

Friday

Find a recording of "your song." Have it playing on the stereo when your partner returns home from work.

Saturday

Love is timeless—and to prove it, cover up all the clocks in your house for the entire weekend. (Remember that one of the best things about being on vacation is the freedom from schedules and clocks and appointments. You can create a mini-vacation by freeing yourself from the tyranny of the clock for 48 hours.)

—————— Week 3 ——————

Sunday

Take the lightbulbs out of the lamps in your bedroom. Replace them with candles. You take it from there . . .

Monday

Head to your local music store. Buy Earl Klugh's *Heartstrings* album, compact disc or tape.

Tuesday

Start the day in a special way. Read an inspirational passage from a favorite book.

Wednesday

End the day in a special way. Give her a massage.

Thursday

Yes—today is gift day! Buy him a wild tie. Buy her a stuffed animal.

Friday

Declare today "Couple's Day," "Wife Appreciation Day," or some such nonsense. Use any excuse to go out on the town tonight!

Saturday

Share a bubble bath.

Week 4

Sunday

Spend all day in bed. Read the Sunday Funnies aloud to her. Make love. Enjoy breakfast in bed. Take a nap. Watch old movies on TV. Make love again. Have Domino's Pizza deliver dinner.

Monday

Call in sick. Repeat yesterday.

Tuesday

Call her from work to tell her you love her . . . *every hour on the hour!*

Wednesday

Pack a picnic lunch. Meet him at work. Close his office door. *Bon appétit!*

Thursday

(*You haven't forgotten what day today is, have you?*) Today's gift won't cost you a dime. Write her a love letter.

Friday

Today's assignment is to find one romantic idea/concept/gift in the newspaper. Act on it within the next two weeks.

Saturday

Make a couple of *incredible* banana splits.

Surprise!

145

Surprises are an integral part of the romantic lifestyle. The everyday and ordinary can be made into the unexpected and special. Surprises come in all shapes and sizes . . . *and* in all budget ranges.

✦ Make up your mind to add surprises to your repertoire.
✦ Think-up two small surprises and one big one.
✦ Plan one surprise for next week; one for next month; one for next year.

146

The surprise get-away weekend is a romantic classic. Take advantage of nearby hotels' special weekend packages (often appropriately called "Marriage-Saver Weekends" or "Lovers' Escape Weekends"); or find a quaint bed-and-breakfast or picturesque inn. Pack bags for both of you, and whisk your partner away upon his or her arrival from work!

147

Buy tickets well in advance to the theatre, symphony, ball game or concert. Don't tell her what the tickets are for . . . simply tell her to mark her calendar. The mystery surrounding the event will be almost as much fun as the event itself. Guaranteed.

148

Surprise Strategy #1: *The Time-Delay Tactic.* Learn what she likes/wants. Get it for her, but hold on to it for a few weeks or months. (This gives her time to forget about it, or think that *you've* forgotten.) Surprise her with it when she least expects it.

149

Surprise Strategy #2: *The Little White Lie*. Setting up surprises involves a subtle touch, a smooth manner and *outright lying*. Don't worry about it. [When it comes to romance, the end justifies the means.]

150

Detail people vs. *overview* people. It will be much easier for you to pull surprises if you're a *detail* person and your partner is an *overview* person. Detail people are good at covering their trail, paying attention to the little things, and acting "normal." Overview people—those who tend to "see the big picture" in life—will not even notice your little slips. If *you're* the over-view person, you'll need to be extra careful when executing surprises. Those detail-oriented partners will notice every unusual phone call, every little change in your schedule, and that mischievous or guilty look on your face.

Become an artist of your relationship.

- GJPG

151-152

☞ Surprise her by bringing dinner home from a gourmet take-out cafe.
☞ Surprise him by making his favorite gourmet dessert.

153

Buy him a puppy. Buy her a kitten.

154

♦ Surprise your partner with an *unexpected* three-day weekend. (Arrange it ahead of time with his or her boss and staff.)

♦ Surprise her by doing one of her chores for her.

155

Surprise her by giving *her* a gift on *your* birthday. First, you'll surprise the heck out of her! Second, you'll experience the truth that "It's as much fun to give as it is to receive."

156

✦ Surprise her by celebrating "Cat in the Hat Day," March 2nd.

✦ Surprise him by celebrating "National Grouch Day," October 15th.

✦ Surprise your lefty lover on August 13th, "Int'l. Lefthanders Day."

✦ Surprise your trivia buff by celebrating "Trivia Day," January 4th.

✦ Keep the surprises coming by getting a copy of an indispensable resource book called *The Day-By-Day Celebration Book,* by John Kremer. With 4,800 listings, you'll be able to find *some* reason to celebrate or take the day off work any day of the year! At bookstores or call 515-472-6130.

157

While out shopping with her: If she's trying on an outfit she *adores* (or that *you* find sexy)—pay for it quickly while she's still in the dressing room. (A good reason to carry *cash* on these little outings.) Return to the dressing room with a pair of scissors, cut off the price tags, and announce that she can wear the outfit out of the store. Watch her jaw drop. Then watch her leap into your arms.

158

While the two of you are out grocery shopping or running errands, have a friend deliver and set-out a gourmet dinner, complete with your best china, candles and soft music. (Don't forget to return the favor.)

Happy Birthday!

159

+ Send **20** stuffed animals to her on her **20**th birthday.
+ Send **30** red roses to him on his **30**th birthday.
+ Send **40** reasons why you love her on her **40**th birthday.
+ Send **50** balloons to him on his **50**th birthday.
+ Send **60** greeting cards to her on her **60**th birthday.
+ Send **70** sunflowers to him on his **70**th birthday.

160

Use sparklers instead of candles on his birthday cake.

161

Send her a birthday card *every day for a month!*

162

On your lover's birthday, send her mother a "Thank You" card.

163

Get *The Oxford Book of Ages*, edited by Anthony and Sally Sampson. It's a great collection of quotes about *every* age—from 0 to 100!

❝Forty is the old age of youth; fifty is the youth of old age.❞

~ Victor Hugo

❝At twenty years of age, the will reigns; at thirty, the wit; and at forty, the judgment.❞

~ Benjamin Franklin

❝The years between fifty and seventy are the hardest. You are always being asked to do things, and yet you are not decrepit enough to turn them down.❞

~ T.S. Eliot

164

How about a video celebration of the year he was born? For just $14.95 you can get a 30-minute taped newsreel, featuring world events, news, personalities, styles and major events from the year of your partner's birth. Call Flik-Baks at 800-541-3533; in California, 310-823-5755. These are the years that are available so far: 1929, 1930, 1932, 1939, 1940, 1941, 1942, 1943, 1949, 1950, 1951, 1952, 1953, 1954, 1955, 1959, 1960, 1961, 1962, 1963, 1964 & 1965.

165

Magazines from the week or month of his birthdate also make great birthday gifts! Try a local used bookstore or call the Avenue Victor Hugo Bookstore, in Boston. They stock *thousands* of magazines, and the people there are great. Call them at 617-266-7746.

166

Convince his boss to call him at home at 7 o'clock on the morning of his birthday—to give him the day off!

"What a coincidence! You forgot my birthday and I forgot how to cook."

167

Get her an actual newspaper from the day she was born! The Historic Newspaper Archives has newspapers from more than 50 U.S. cities, including *The New York Times, The Wall Street Journal,* and *The Los Angeles Times.* These are authentic, well-preserved editions of the entire original newspapers! Call 800-221-3221; in New Jersey, 908-381-2332.

➤ For the newspaper itself: $39.50   ➤ With presentation case: $75

168

Find and record a bunch of "birthday" and "age-related" songs for him or her. Like "You Say It's Your Birthday" from the Beatles' *White Album.* And how about their song "When I'm Sixty-Four" from *Sergeant Pepper's Lonely Hearts Club Band?* Here are a few more birthday songs . . .

♪✷ *Happy Birthday,* Stevie Wonder
♪✷ *Happy Birthday,* New Kids On The Block
♪✷ *Happy Birthday,* Altered Images
♪✷ *Happy Birthday To You,* Bing Crosby
♪✷ *Happy Birthday To You,* Eddy Howard
♪✷ *Happy Birthday To You,* Sunsetters
♪✷ *Young At Heart,* Frank Sinatra
♪✷ *I Wish I Were 18 Again,* George Burns

169

Declare it your lover's "Birthday *Month,*" and do something special every day for the 30 days preceding THE day. Write a love note every day (and hide it somewhere). Or create a series of "themed" gifts, using the number of years that he or she will be celebrating. Or create a little evening ritual. Or . . .

170

•→ Send him one birthday card for each year of his age—*one-a-day for as long as it takes.*
•→ Send him one birthday card for each year of his age—*all at one time!*

171

And if you're not satisfied with celebrating once a year, you can always celebrate *half-birthdays* every six months!

Celebrate!

172

→ Romantic arithmetic: Champagne = Celebration.

→ Today's homework: Pick up a bottle of Korbel on the way home from work . . . pop the cork with your lover . . . celebrate!

173

Buy a case of champagne. Label each of the 12 bottles . . .

1. *His birthday*
2. *Her birthday*
3. *Christmas/Hanukkah*
4. *Your anniversary (of meeting or marrying)*
5. *Groundhog Day*
6. *For a midnight snack*
7. *Before making love*
8. *Celebrate a great accomplishment at work*
9. *Mozart's Birthday*
10. *The first snowfall*
11. *For making up after a fight*
12. *The first day of Spring*

174

Balloons! Balloon bouquets. Helium-filled balloons. Heart-shaped red balloons. Mickey Mouse/Snoopy/Garfield balloons. Silvery, shiny mylar balloons. Giant-sized balloons. Balloons with your names on them. Balloons with personalized messages on them. Look in your local Yellow Pages under . . . "Balloons."

175

New Year's Eve in Times Square!

176

Have you made your plans for the two New Year's Eve celebrations to end all New Year's Eve celebrations? I'm talking about the next millennium! It's coming soon! When the calendar changes to the year 2000, and then to 2001, the planet's going to party like never before. Start planning!

177

❋ Celebrate all of the basics (birthdays, anniversaries, holidays and Valentine's Day), and then . . .

❋ Celebrate other special, crazy or unique occasions. These are a few of the occasions that some members of the Romance Class celebrate:

➤ Beethoven's birthday: December 16th
➤ "Full Moon Day"
➤ The spring and autumn Equinox
➤ The winter and summer Solstice
➤ "Hug Day" (Leo Buscaglia's birthday!—March 31st)
➤ "First Snowfall Day" (A good excuse to skip work!)
➤ First spring day over 70 degrees
➤ Oprah Winfrey's birthday: January 29th
➤ Payday!
➤ National Kazoo Day: January 28th
➤ Temporary Insanity Day: February 19th
➤ National Goof-Off Day: March 22nd
➤ Relationship Renewal Day: May 3rd
➤ Garfield's birthday: June 19th
➤ National Puzzle Day: July 13th
➤ Kiss-And-Make-Up Day: August 25th
➤ Snoopy's birthday: October 2nd
➤ Sweetest Day: October 16th
➤ Mickey Mouse's birthday: November 18th
➤ National Whiner's Day: December 26th

Valentine's Day

178

Valentine's Day is *not* the most romantic day of the year. [You *still* have to recognize it and act on it—but you *don't* get any extra credit for it, guys.] Valentine's Day is one of those *Obligatory Romance* days.

179

Don't buy roses on Valentine's Day! It's common, expected and expensive.

✳ Buy *different* flowers.
✳ Or exercise your creativity: Do something unique, quirky or touching.
✳ Write a poem . . . or copy one from a book of poetry.
✳ Write a love letter.

180

Turn Valentine's Day into a *real* holiday: Take the day off work! Spend the day in bed. Go to the movies. Go out to dinner. Go dancing. Take a drive. Make love. Go for a stroll.

181

Mail him a Valentine's Day card. Mail him 20! Make your own card. Make a *huge* card. Send a musical greeting card—available in most card shops for just a few bucks!

182

❦ Send her a box filled with those Valentine Conversation Heart candies. A **BIG** box.

❦ Use Valentine Conversation Heart candies to spell-out a romantic message to her. Leave it on the kitchen table or paste it to a piece of construction paper.

❦ Replace all the Cheerios with Valentine Conversation Hearts.

183

☞ Celebrate by going to see the most romantic musical on Broadway: *The Phantom of the Opera*, at the Majestic Theatre, 247 West 44th Street, New York City. Call 212-239-6200 for tickets.

☞ Or, just get the CD. Very melodramatic, mysterious and romantic!

184

Greet him at the front door wearing a big red ribbon—and nothing else. (This also makes an inexpensive—and *always appreciated*—birthday or anniversary gift!)

185

Keep your eyes open for pre-Valentine's Day articles in magazines and newspapers. Rip out the articles, circle the best ideas, and plan accordingly. (And don't forget to *keep those articles for future reference!*)

186

St. Valentine's Day mid-winter carnivals are held in these cities:

❄ St. Paul, Minnesota
❄ Quebec City, Canada
❄ Venice, Italy

Bundle up, then hop in your car or call your travel agent to make plans.

187

Use kids' valentines: A whole box full of silly puns and clichés, all for just a couple of bucks.

✴ Mail a boxful of 'em.   ✴ Fill the sink with them.
✴ Fill his briefcase full of them.   ✴ Fill her pillow with them.
✴ Tape them all over her car.   ✴ Mail one-a-day for a month.

188

For future reference: Buy an *extra* bag of Valentine Conversation Heart candies and save them for use six months later.

*Beware of
"Relationship Entropy"—
The tendency of relationships to become more
diffuse if not cared-for and
nurtured; the tendency for once-close lovers to drift
apart if both of them don't work at it.*

~ GJPG

Little Things Mean a Lot

189

Call her from work for no other reason than to tell her "I love you." Make it a habit.

190

Prescription for Romance # 1: Compliment her. Repeat every 4 to 6 hours.

191

Look—no, *gaze*— into her eyes more often.

✦ Women are very eye-oriented.

✦ You know, they say that one's eyes are a "window into one's soul." [Maybe that's why it's so hard to look people in the eye when you lie.]

192

Prescription for Romance #2: Say "I love you" at least three times today. Repeat dosage every day for the rest of your life.

193

Write him a little love note; insert it in the book he's reading.

194

Prescription for Romance #3: Hug. Often!

195

Brush her hair for her. Be gentle.

✳ Several couples in the Romance Class have turned hair-brushing into a nightly ritual. They report that it provides them with a great time to relax at the end of the day, spend time alone together, and talk.

196

Prescription for Romance #4: Run your hands under hot water before coming to bed (!)

197

Give him a T-shirt featuring his favorite cartoon character.

198

Prescription for Romance #5: On Monday, place a single flower on the kitchen table. On Tuesday, place a different flower on her pillow. On Wednesday place a flower in the sink. On Thursday . . .

199

Bring home her favorite:

✓ Ice cream
✓ Cookies
✓ Magazine

✓ Classic movie on video
✓ Flower
✓ "Penny candy"

200

Prescription for Romance #6: Indulge in your lover's hobby, sport or passion. Buy him a new golf club. Buy her a new tennis racket. Rent his favorite movie. Get a gallon of her favorite ice cream.

Actions Speak Louder Than Words

201

Cuddle up in front of a roaring fire. (No TV. No kids. No phone.)

202

Carve her initials and yours in a tree.

203

Leave a trail of your clothes, leading from the front door to your bedroom.

204

Change one bad habit! Preferably the one that she's been nagging you about. [You've known all along that she's right, of course.] Actually, you'll probably benefit more than she will! Stop smoking! Drop 10 pounds! Get yourself some nice clothes!

205

Fill a basin with hot water. Take off his shoes and socks for him. Sit him down in his favorite chair. Wash his feet. Let them soak for 10 minutes. Dry off his feet. Resume life as before.

206

Hug. Cuddle. Snuggle. Touch. Stroke.

(In 1985 Ann Landers asked her readers: "Would you be content to be held close and treated tenderly and forget about 'the act'?" She was swamped with 100,000 replies within four days, with 72 percent of them saying "yes," they would be content to just snuggle.)

207

"Spontaneous Celebrations."

* Occasions: It's Tuesday! It's a sunny day! Girlfriend Appreciation Day! Favorite-Number Day! Hug Day!
* Props: Confetti. Champagne. Balloons. Pizza. Candles. Candy.

208

Call your lover on the phone. Make up a lovesong *on the spot* and sing it to her! Make up a tune, make up the words—and just keep singing! (You'll generate laughter, if not appreciation!)

The essence of romance is communication.

~ GJPG

It's Not *What* You Do, But *How You Do It*

209

Don't just walk into the house tonight like you always do . . . Pause on the porch . . . ring the doorbell . . . and greet her with a rose and a bottle of champagne.

210

Get extra-nice wrapping paper and fancy bows. If you truly have two left thumbs, get the store or a neighbor to do your giftwrapping for you. *Never* give a gift without wrapping it.

211

One woman in the Romance Class told us that her husband always manages to incorporate her favorite teddy bear into his many gift presentations.

* He's given her diamond earrings by putting them on the bear's ears.
* He's strung pearls around the bear's neck.
* He's packed the bear inside boxes along with other gifts.
* He's put funny notes in the bear's paw.

212

Strings of pearls have been known to appear inside real oyster shells at fancy restaurants.

213

Strings of pearls have also been presented to the tune of "A String of Pearls" by Glenn Miller.

214

And many diamond rings seem to find their way to the bottom of a glass of champagne.

215

Of course you know how to kiss, but perhaps a refresher course might add a little spark to your lives. Pick up a copy of a fun little book called *The Art of Kissing*, by William Cane. In it are instructions for (among other things) . . .

❧ The Candy Kiss	❧ The Music Kiss	❧ The Perfume Kiss
❧ The Sliding Kiss	❧ The Surprise Kiss	❧ The French Kiss
❧ The Counter Kiss	❧ The Vacuum Kiss	❧ The Japanese Kiss

216

Perhaps you need therapy. *Hug Therapy.* That's the title of another fun little book, this one by Kathleen Keating. In it are instructions for . . .

- The Bear Hug
- The Grabber-Squeezer Hug
- The Heart-Centered Hug
- The Sandwich Hug
- The Back-To-Front Hug
- The Custom-Tailored Hug
- The Cheek Hug

217

Put a written message *inside* a balloon. If you can't find a clear balloon, use a regular one: Insert the message, then attach a pin to the string.

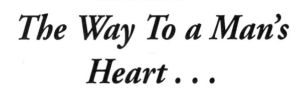

The Way To a Man's Heart . . .

218

The title of this chapter is a bit of a misnomer, as I've found that women are *at least* as food-oriented as men are. So we can safely say that one of the best ways to *anyone's* heart is through his or her stomach. *Bon appétit!*

219

You can spice up *any* meal at home—from gourmet extravaganzas to TV dinners—by adding candlelight and soft music. Don't wait for "special occasions" or for weekends, to bring out the romance.

220

❦ If your lover is a tea lover, get her a subscription to the "Upton Tea Quarterly" newsletter. It includes listings and information on 150 varieties of fine loose tea. Write to Upton Tea Imports, 231 South Street, Upton, Massachusetts 01748.

❦ If she's into coffee, see the chapter titled "1-800-ROM-ANCE" for details on The Coffee Connection's subscription service!

221

Why not splurge, and hire a caterer to prepare a special meal *just for the two of you*? This way, you'll both have more time to relax, perhaps take a bubble bath together, and avoid dealing with pots and pans!

222

What's her all-time favorite meal? Learn to make it! Get help from friends, neighbors or relatives—whatever it takes.

223

Create an "At-Home Date": Includes dinner and dancing. Formal attire required.

224

The way to his stomach often involves directions to his favorite restaurant. Do you know his all-time favorite restaurant; favorite diner; favorite fast food joint; favorite fancy restaurant; favorite pizza parlor?

☞ See the chapter titled "Dining Out" for more suggestions.

225

If your guy is a true beer fanatic, you'll want to schedule a visit to "The Disneyland of Beer": The American Museum of Brewing History and Arts, in Fort Mitchell, Kentucky. It's a sort of hall of fame for suds lovers! The museum is part of a complex that includes the Oldenberg Brewery, a micro brewery making several German style beers. Housed in the museum is the world's largest collection of beer and brewing memorabilia. Yikes! Call 606-341-2800, and ask for the beer museum.

226

Beer lovers will appreciate *la biere amoureuse*—that's French for "Love Beer." That's what Fischer Brewery of France calls its "36.15 brew." Check with your local importer or visit France!

227

For a sensual, silly time:

✶ Blindfold her.
✶ Sit her on the floor next to the refrigerator.
✶ Feed her a variety of delicious foods: Strawberries, Hershey's Chocolate Kisses, cherry tomatoes, cheese, ice cream, Cheerios, cookies, popcorn, yogurt, watermelon, leftover chicken, pickles, olives, maple syrup, etc.
✶ (There's a great scene like this in the movie *9 1/2 Weeks*.)

228

Get the pizza chef to arrange the pepperoni in the shape of a heart.

229

Go in search of "The Perfect Pizza." It could take you months or years, and you might gain 10 pounds—but if your lover is a pizza fiend, it will all be worth it!

230

Embark on a series of "Restaurant Discoveries": Each week go to a different restaurant. Choose a restaurant "theme" that appeals to both of you, for instance:

✦ Find the best French restaurant in town.
✦ Find the best diner in the state.
✦ Mix-and-match all the ethnic restaurants: Chinese, Mexican, Greek, Thai, Italian, Japanese, etc.

Love will make a way out of no way.

~ Lynda Barry

231

How about outrageous, home-made muffins—by mail!? Suzanne's Mail Order Muffins makes 'em from ingredients including fresh fruits, Grand Marnier, Bacardi rum and Ghiradelli chocolate! Sounds good to me! Call for a free gift catalog: 800-742-2403.

232

Aphrodisiacs!?

Wondrous claims have been made about a great variety of foods, from oysters and chocolate to basil and green **m&m**'s. Personally, I feel that it's the *mood and environment* surrounding the presentation of the food that determines the potential amorous conclusion of the evening.

But by all means, try some exotic recipes. Hey, it couldn't hurt!

And regardless of whether or not certain foods can chemically make one more interested in love, there's always the scientifically proven "Placebo Effect," which indicates that the mere *belief* in the power of an agent can bring about the believed-in effect. This means that virtually *any* food could potentially be an aphrodisiac.

*Because romantic moments are charged
with emotion
they create positive memories that
last a lifetime.*

~ GJPG

233

When you're in a hurry—but have had your fill of fast food, pizza and Chinese take-out—find an "over-the-counter gourmet" shop. They're becoming more popular as our lives get busier. Also known as "guilt-free take-out," you can get quality, nutritional meals that are virtually hassle-free. This means that you can devote *even more* of your energy to creating the romantic atmosphere and to paying attention to your *lover* instead of your *oven*.

234

Write a *thank-you* note to James McNair for writing the book *Pizza*. It's the only cookbook I've ever opened, much less used, and it's allowed me to partake in the mysteries of the kitchen—to the delight (and surprise!) of my wife. This book is great for beginners, as it explains all the basics; and it's great for connoisseurs, too, as it includes some truly amazing and exotic recipes, including:

➤ French Style Pizza (Pissaladiere) ➤ Kung Pao Shrimp Pizza
➤ Smoked Salmon & Brie Pizza ➤ Thai Chicken Pizza
➤ Mixed Seafood Pizza ➤ The BLT Pizza
➤ Barbecued Chicken Pizza ➤ The Smoked Pheasant Pizza

The book also includes delicious photographs of each completed pizza, so novices like me will know if we even come close!

235

Wine is the perfect complement to any nice meal. Find a wine you both enjoy. Buy a case of it and reserve it just for the two of you. You could start a delicious and slightly intoxicating personal tradition.

For some free, down-to-earth advice on wines, give Martin Block a call at 617-337-2134. [He advises me on *my* selections, and said I could give-out his number. He owns one of the finest little spirit shops in New England—*Michael's.*]

236

Take a wine tasting course together.

Erotica

237

Let's start with the basics: Do you *know* what your partner considers erotic? Or do you *assume* you know? Do you figure she likes what your *last* girlfriend enjoyed? Do you think he's just like the guy described in last month's *Cosmo*? Do you believe everything you read in *Penthouse Letters*??

✳ Talk about what each of you considers erotic.

✳ Set your inhibitions and judgments aside. (Maybe warm-up with a little champagne.)

✳ Give yourselves plenty of time to explore this fun, complicated, frustrating-but-rewarding aspect of being human.

238

Go lingerie shopping together. [Accompany her into the dressing room.]

239

Humbly submitted for your perusal:

∿ *Little Birds,* by Anaïs Nin
∿ *Delta of Venus,* also by Anaïs Nin
∿ *Lady Chatterley's Lover,* by D.H. Lawrence
∿ *Tropic of Cancer,* by Henry Miller
∿ *Tropic of Capricorn,* also by Henry Miller
∿ *Yellow Silk,* edited by Lily Pond & Richard Russo

240

For women: Fulfill a fantasy: Greet him at the door wearing high heels, garter belt and stockings. [As the Nike ads say, "Just do it."]

241

For men: Fulfill a fantasy: Become her vision of Prince Charming...whether it involves dressing in a tuxedo or in a sexy tank-top T-shirt and hardhat! Indulge her.

242

Get a copy of the *Kama Sutra*. Read parts of it aloud to each other. Try some of its suggestions.

243

Get a copy of *The Joy of Sex*. Same thing as above.

244

Kiss every square inch of her body . . . S-L-O-W-L-Y.

245

"Christen" every room in your house or apartment by making love in it. (Don't forget to include the stairways and closets. The more adventurous among you may want to include the porches and backyard, too.)

246

One man in the Romance Class told us how an accidental wine spill resulted in an erotic tradition celebrated regularly with his wife. She spilled a glass of wine on her new silk blouse. Instead of being upset, she thought about it for a second, grabbed *his* wine glass, emptied it down the front of her blouse, and said, "If you want it, come and get it!" (They've since graduated to cordials!)

247

When he's traveling on business, give him a sexy wake-up call at 6 a.m.

248

When choosing erotic movies . . . it may be helpful to remember that men and women often have different definitions of "erotic." Women like the smoldering passion of *The Bridges of Madison County*. For men, you can pretty much sum up their taste in erotic movies in two words: Nude blonde. *(Basic Instinct. 9 1/2 Weeks. Body Double.)* [Just *trying* to be helpful!]

249

Armchair lovers might prefer their erotica at home and in prose. You might consider subscribing to *Libido Magazine*—"Erotica for people who like to read." You can get a sample issue for $8. A subscription to the quarterly publication is $30. Write to P.O. Box 146721, Chicago, Illinois 60614.

250

Before you leave on a trip, leave a bottle of scented massage oil on the night stand, along with a note saying "I'm going to use this entire bottle on you as soon as I return." (Then, make good on your promise!)

251

Massages come in two varieties: Sensual and sexual. Learn the subtle—but important—differences. One will relax your partner and put her to sleep. The other will . . . well—do the opposite!

252

Slang alert! *Jeepin'* means having sex in the back seat of a car. (Vocabulary lessons in *school* were never so helpful!)

253

For more information on massage:

☞ *The Massage Book,* by George Downing
☞ *Massage: Principles & Techniques,* by Gertrude Beard & Elizabeth Wood
☞ Playboy has these massage videotapes available: *Secrets of EuroMassage, Ultimate Massage,* and *Erotic Massage.* They're informative, sensual, and available in many video rental shops or by calling the Playboy Catalog at 800-423-9494.

Exotica

254

One of the most exotic places in the world you could *possibly* visit is Nepal—the tiny Asian country where Mount Everest resides. Trekking through the Himalayas with your lover will rejuvenate and inspire both of you! [I took a two-week trek recently, and it was one of the highlights of my life!]

Trekking adventures that last from several days to several weeks are available, and start around $2,500. The expert on trekking in Nepal (and in trekking vacations to other countries as well) is Steve Conlon, founder of Above the Clouds Trekking. [Isn't that a *fabulous* name for a company?!] Call him at 800-233-4499; in Massachusetts call 508-799-4499, or write to P.O. Box 398, Worcester, Massachusetts 01602.

255

Kauai, "The Garden Isle" of the Hawaiian Islands, is also known as "The Honeymoon Island." 'Nuff said!

256

If you'd rather ride than walk, consider a trip on the Trans-Siberian Railroad in a vintage private train! You'll travel in original antique carriages that were once part of the fabled Orient Express. The train has *three* dining cars, a cozy bar/lounge, and even a special shower car! The 17-day program includes three days in Beijing and two in Moscow—and runs close to $7,000. Call TCS Expeditions at 800-727-7477, or write 2025 First Avenue, Suite 830, Seattle, Washington 98121. (They also operate private train trips along the ancient Silk Road, through China and Central Asia, and across the U.S. on the *American Orient Express*.)

257

➤ How about a balloon adventure over Switzerland? Or France. Or Italy. Or Turkey. Or Austria. Call Bombard Balloon Adventures at 800-862-8537, or write to 855 Donald Ross Road, Juno Beach, Florida 33408.

➤ And once you get hooked on ballooning, you'll want to know about "In The Air: The Ultimate Catalog for Balloon Enthusiasts"! Call them at 800-583-8038.

258

If you'd rather ride—on a horse—call Equitour, which organizes horseback vacations as far afield as India and Australia. Trips through the American Wild West are also available, of course. The trips are wonderfully diverse: On the Wyoming trip (which follows the Oregon Trail and Pony Express routes) you camp out in tents; while on the Vermont trip you stay in quaint country inns. Call Equitour at 800-545-0019.

259

Info on exotic tours of many countries is just a free phone call away!

•+ Germany—800-248-9539
•+ Switzerland—800-662-0021
•+ France—800-237-2747
•+ Ireland—800-223-6470
•+ Monaco—800-753-9696
•+ Scandinavia—800-346-4636

260

Create your own "Fantasy Vacation." What's your lover's idea of the Perfect, Ultimate, Wonderful, Fantasy Vacation? Let your imagination run wild. Keep the dream alive over the years by collecting brochures, posters and books on your Fantasy Vacation location. (Someday, you just might make the dream come true . . .)

Romance on a Budget

261

Where to get inexpensive flowers:

✦ Supermarkets ✦ Street vendors ✦ Meadows ✦ Your own garden ✦

262

Timing is *everything*, when it comes to saving a few bucks. You could save 20% to 50% on virtually every gift you buy if you shop smart . . .

★ Hit the stores immediately after Christmas.
★ Shop at end-of-the-season sales.
★ Look for overstock sales.
★ Scan catalogs regularly, looking for deals.

263

Go to vacation spots off-season.

264

Buy camping equipment instead of going on an expensive vacation. A one-time outlay will assure you of years of inexpensive vacations. (You'll also be prepared for last-minute vacationing opportunities and quickie weekend get-aways.)

265

Most cities have "City Coupon Books" that include hundreds of discount coupons for restaurants, shops and services. These coupon books usually cost just a few bucks, and can save you hundreds of dollars *if you use them!* They're also a good incentive to get the two of you out of the house, and get out of that rut you've been in!

ⵍⵍⵍⵍⵍⵍⵍⵍⵍⵍⵍⵍⵍⵍⵍⵍⵍⵍ

Hmm—1001 ways to be romantic, eh?
Let's see . . . If I use one idea per day,
this book will last me 2.75 years.
At one idea per week, that's 19.25 years!

ⵍⵍⵍⵍⵍⵍⵍⵍⵍⵍⵍⵍⵍⵍⵍⵍⵍⵍ

266

Rediscover coffeehouses! They're an inexpensive and entertaining change of pace. (Folk music never really dies, it just continuously ebbs and flows.)

267

Playbill Magazine, which accompanies most theatre productions, often advertises a "Show-of-the-Month Club." Good prices, good seats, and a good way to have something to look forward to.

268

Buy *season tickets* instead of two-tickets-at-a-time for shows and events that you attend. You'll save money in the long run, you'll get better seats, and you'll go out more! Box seats are great—whether they're at the ballgame or the ballet!

269

Many symphonies and theatres have discount tickets available on the day-of, or evening-of, performances. If your partner doesn't mind a little uncertainty, this is a great way to save a few bucks and still enjoy an evening of culture and entertainment.

270

Shopping for romance and shopping for bargains can sometimes mean the same thing—*if* you know where to shop! Every town has its fun, quirky little shops. Many towns also have Target stores, where "everyday low prices" is more than just a slogan. They've got everything from champagne glasses to lingerie, and lots of practical stuff for guys! It's a great resource for stocking your Gift Closet! (See #48.)

271

Close to home, you could re-discover community theatres. They're fun, inexpensive and entertaining. Many small cities and towns have truly excellent community theatres. Call them today for a schedule of upcoming shows. Don't forget to call a number of near-by towns, too!

272

(Victoria's Secret has *great* end-of-season sales. Call 800-888-8200 for a catalog . . . or visit their nearest shop.)

273

Buy wine and champagne *by the case*. You'll typically get a 10% to 20% discount off the per-bottle price. You'll save money, and always have a bottle on hand for those "Spontaneous Celebrations."

Spare No Expense

274

Maybe he'd like to fly the Concorde. A one-way ticket to Europe is just a tad over $4,200.

275

Why not hire a private Lear Jet, and take your lover to dinner in another city?! (He deserves to be treated like a king, doesn't he?) Call Executive Jet Aviation at 800-848-6436; in Ohio, 614-237-0363. Or check your local Yellow Pages under "Airlines" or "Aircraft Charter/Rental/Leasing Services."

276

Or how about a fine vintage wine from the year of your lover's birth—or the year of your anniversary? The Antique Wine Company of Great Britain Ltd., has a huge wine cellar of aged fine wines, dating back to 1893. Their specialty is the "Birthday Vintage Gift": A vintage wine presented in a satin-lined, leather-finish case with an engraved plaque for your personal message, plus an original *London Times* newspaper from the day of the individual's birth—delivered by personal courier. The value of each gift depends on the year. Prices start at $450. Call 800-827-7153.

277

You *could* update his *entire* album collection! Convert his aging album collection of beloved Beatles albums, Moody Blues tunes and Rolling Stones records to compact discs. Converting a lifetime collection of 500-some albums would cost about $6,500.

278

Dinner at The Wild Boar Restaurant, in Nashville, Tennessee. A wine list that fills 100 pages and includes 3,000 selections, with a total inventory of 12,000 bottles. Eighteen-karat gold table settings. A $2 million art collection (a feast for your eyes) . . . oh, and good food, too. Call 615-329-1313.

279

The hands-down winner in the "Spare No Expense" category is the *three week vacation trip around the world on the Concorde.* The trip is offered only once each year, with space limited to 96 people. Here's a brief look at the itinerary (cities may change from year-to-year):

* You're flown first-class to Dallas, where you pick-up the Concorde . . .
* You head for Honolulu for two nights . . .
* Then on to Sydney, Australia for three nights . . .
* And Hong Kong for three nights . . .
* Then Delhi, India . . . Nairobi, Kenya . . . Cairo, Egypt . . .
* And finally London, then back home.

Each stop includes premier hotel accommodations, gourmet meals, and hand-picked coordinators to help you in any way possible. The cost? Just $50,800 per person.

The tour operator is INTRAV, a specialist in deluxe world travel. (They also run less expensive trips—averaging $3,400—to all seven continents.) Call 800-456-8100 or 314-727-0500, or write to INTRAV at 7711 Bonhomme Avenue, St. Louis, Missouri 63105.

280

And don't forget about:

☆ Caviar
☆ Antique fountain pens
☆ Mink teddy bears

☆ Diamond earrings, rings, & things
☆ 24-karat gold *anything*
☆ Best seat tickets to anything

Basics

281-292

❤ Flowers
❤ Candy
❤ Chocolate!
❤ The simple gold chain
❤ Greeting cards (store-bought)
❤ Greeting cards (home-made)

❤ Jewelry
❤ Teddy bears
❤ Lingerie
❤ Love poems
❤ Lovesongs
❤ Love Coupons

293-304

☙ Love letters
☙ Surprises!
☙ "I love you" phone calls
☙ Romantic dinners in—
   at home by candlelight
☙ Sending flowers to the office
☙ Movies in—with a video

☙ Breakfast in bed
☙ Anniversary celebrations
☙ Weekend get-aways
☙ Romantic dinners out—
   at your favorite cozy restaurant
☙ Ballroom dancing
☙ Movies out—to the theatre

Bubblebaths ○

305

Start simple. Run her a bubble bath.

❧ Unless you already know her favorite type of bath bubbles, simply buy *any* kind. Mr. Bubble will do for starters.

❧ Note: A good steaming bath will stay hot for more than an hour. This gives you plenty of time to run it, then run—leaving her alone to enjoy the surprise and a little privacy.

306

After you've gone through the basics a few times, choose a special evening and *make a big production of it!* Run the bath. Add candles. Garnish with cheese and fruit. Provide champagne. And a book to read. Then get rid of the kids, and make yourself scarce until it's time to towel her off.

307

Be waiting for him in the bathtub when he returns from work.

308

Test your agility—make love in the bathtub. If your tub is simply too small, spread towels on the floor and improvise!

309

Towel her dry after she showers. S-L-O-W-L-Y.

310

A *wintertime* bath suggestion: *Warm her towel in the dryer!* She'll adore you for at least a week afterward.

311

Write her a love letter or a poem. Roll it up and stick it in a bottle. Cork it. Float the bottle in the bathtub.

312

(Baths aren't for women only!)

313

For a touch of class . . . add European soaps and other bath luxuries. A great resource is Katherine March Ltd., a mail order firm specializing in soaps, gels, foams, oils, lotions and more—all imported from Europe. Katherine personally selects all items for their unique ingredients, their beneficial qualities, and their special charm, appearance or history. Call 800-87-MARCH, or write Post Office Box 51844, Durham, North Carolina 27717.

314

Run a bath for her while she's out running errands. Put a candle, a glass of wine, and a bottle of fancy bubble bath on the kitchen table—along with a note saying, "I'll put the groceries away for you. Go relax. You deserve it. I love you."

CreAtive *Notes*

315

Write her a note, poem or letter on one sheet of paper. Glue it to thin cardboard. Cut it up into puzzle-shaped pieces. Mail all the pieces to her in an envelope. Or . . . mail one puzzle piece a day for a week.

316

Write *"I love you"* on the bathroom mirror with a piece of soap.

317

Write notes on rolls of toilet paper; on balloons; on notes inserted *inside* balloons; in the dust on his coffee table; in his appointment calendar; in the margins of her *Cosmopolitan Magazine.*

318

Hide 25 little love notes all over the house. Write short romantic notes on index cards, Post-It Notes, or construction paper cut into little hearts. Then hide them *everywhere:* In the *TV Guide,* in pants pockets, in desk drawers, in socks, under magazines, behind pillows, in the tub, in the refrigerator, in the freezer, in the medicine cabinet, in books, in her briefcase, in his car, in the silverware drawer. Some of these notes may remain hidden for months—or even years. So much the better!

319

Put notes on various household products:

* Joy dishwashing liquid: "Every day with you is a Joy."
* Cheerios: "Just knowing you love me cheers me up!"
* Anything by Old Spice: "You spice up my life!"
* Ritz Crackers: "Let's 'Put On The Ritz' tonight! Let's go dancing!"
* A roll of Lifesavers: "You're a lifesaver!".
* Caress soap: "This is what I'm going to do to you tonight."

320

* Mail him a pack of matches. Attach a note: "I'm hot for you."
* Send her a copy of your resumé. Attach a note: "I want you to get to know me better."
* Mail him a pair of your sexiest panties. Attach a note . . .
* Give him a toy, wind-up telephone. Attach a note: "E.T. phone home—more often!"

321

Send a telegram! Call Western Union at 800-325-6000.

322

✗ Draw funny faces on the eggs in the refrigerator.
✗ Get a local artist to draw a caricature of your own smiling face on some eggs! (Look in the Yellow Pages under "Entertainment" or "Graphic Designers.")

323

Do you remember "passing notes" in school? Do you remember how to fold them up so they tuck into a neat little square? *Well . . . ?!*

324

Cut-out interesting/suggestive/unusual/funny headlines from the daily newspapers. When you've collected about 25 of them, simply dump them in an envelope and mail them to your lover.

☞ The last batch I sent to my wife included these headlines:

- ✛ WHAT'S THE KEY TO A GOOD MARRIAGE?
- ✛ ARE WE CRACKING UNDER THE STRAIN?
- ✛ SEX AFTER MARRIAGE?
- ✛ STILL GONZO AFTER ALL THESE YEARS
- ✛ MUCH ADO ABOUT CHEESECAKE
- ✛ JUST ONE OF THOSE CRAZY THINGS
- ✛ A PERFECT 10!
- ✛ GIFTS MIGHT EASE THE PAIN
- ✛ TALES OF INTRIGUE, ACTION AND ROMANCE

325

Put notes/flowers/candy on his car windshield. (See the chapter on "Cars" for further ideas.)

326

Let comics speak for you! Tape them to the refrigerator. Hide them in her purse. Hide them in her briefcase. Pack them in his suitcase. . .

- ❋ Blondie and Dagwood's marriage issues
- ❋ Cathy's dating dilemmas
- ❋ Charlie Brown's unrequited love
- ❋ Lucy's chasing Schroeder; Sally's chasing Linus
- ❋ The Far Side's . . . well, uh . . . just plain funny and weird situations
- ❋ Brenda Starr's ill-fated love affairs

Custom Made

327

Would you like your life to read like a romance novel? Well now it *can!* You can get a romance novel customized with you and your lover as the hero and heroine. Two titles are available: *Another Day in Paradise* and *Love's Bounty.* Each book will include more than 20 personal details about the two of you. Only $29.95! Call Beach House Presentations at 800-444-3356.

328

Jim Rickert, "The Songsmith" will write and record original songs for you. (This guy is *really great.*) Tell him the type/style of song you want, the theme, occasion, and specific information you want included—and he'll customize an original melody that your lover is sure to love. He can give you songs that range from a solo singer accompanied by a guitar, to a singer with full orchestration!

✦ The quickest and least expensive option is to choose one of his original melodies from a catalog of styles (rock, ballad, country, folk, reggae, etc.); then fill-out a questionnaire that will allow him to customize the song with names, dates and personal references. He'll record the song, with full orchestration, for just $43.

✦ He can also write entirely new lyrics for you, or set your words to music. This service starts at $72.

✦ He can also compose entirely new music from scratch for you, and record it simply or elaborately. This service starts at $150, and the final cost depends on the level of sophistication you're seeking.

Normal turn-around time is about two weeks. Call him at 617-471-8500, or write to The Creative Works/Songsmith, 49 Centre Street, Quincy, Massachusetts 02129.

329

The most unbelievably beautiful calligraphy flows from the pen of Maria Thomas, who runs Pendragon, Ink. I've seen lots of calligraphy through the years, but when I saw the work she did for me, I was absolutely stunned. When you want custom calligraphy to enhance . . .

- ∾ A poem
- ∾ A love note
- ∾ A love letter
- ∾ Verses from a favorite song
- ∾ A scroll
- ∾ A frameable quote
- ∾ A certificate
- ∾ Wedding vows
- ∾ Wedding invitations

Call Maria Thomas or Carolyne Baron at 508-234-6843; or fax your copy directly to 508-234-5446; or mail it to 27 Prospect Street, Whitinsville, Massachusetts 01588. They're fast, friendly and experienced—with 30 years of flowing script behind them!

330

Do-it-yourself: *Custom made Chinese fortune cookies!* Buy a batch of them at a local Chinese/Oriental grocery store (or get some from your favorite Chinese restaurant). Pull out their fortunes and insert your own! From silly to sexy, from playful to profound, you decide!

331

If your lover is also a wine lover, why not surprise her with some quality California wines bottled with *custom labels?* Windsor Vineyards will print three lines of custom copy onto their specially-designed labels for you. They can also reproduce artwork that you send them—so get creative! And, you can order as few as three bottles. Call them at 800-214-9463 or 415-435-3113, in Tiburon, California.

332

Visualize a custom-created cartoon/animal/human/fantasy character as a "soft sculpture" doll, and you'll come close to picturing the wonderful creatures that Lisa Lichtenfels creates. Everything she makes is a one-of-a-kind, whimsical piece of plush artwork. She specializes in fantasy figures— people as butterflies, women as mermaids, plus animals and mythical beasts—as well as realistic-looking people in miniature or in life-sized versions (patterned after photos supplied by customers). Lisa is a former animator for Disney Studios, who's been doing custom work for more than 10 years. Her creations are true works of art, and generally cost a couple thousand dollars, depending on the size and detailing. Write to her at Post Office Box 90537, Springfield, Massachusetts 01109.

333

If she's a one-of-a-kind woman, why not present her with a one-of-a-kind piece of jewelry? Check the Yellow Pages under "Jewelry Designers."

334

Does your lover deserve to be on the front cover of *Playmate Magazine?* Should your wife or fiancée be pictured on the front of *Modern Bride?* Should the two of you be featured on the cover of *Together Magazine?* How about *Psychology Today, Skiing Magazine, Car and Driver* or *Celebrity?*

All you have to do is send a snapshot and $19.95 (plus $4.95 for shipping) to Celebrity Photos, Inc., and they'll print a custom cover for you, insert it in an 8-by-10-inch Lucite frame, and deliver it to you in just three weeks. (Yes, you get your original snapshot returned to you.)

Other magazine covers include:

* *National Lampoon*
* *The Artist's Magazine*
* *Baby's World*
* *Musician Magazine*
* *Popular Photography*
* *Inc. Magazine*
* *Cycle World*
* *Teen Scene*
* *Boating Magazine*

* *Yachting*
* *Parents Magazine*
* *Flying*
* *Writer's Digest*
* *Sport*
* *Bartender Magazine*
* *Computer Life*
* *Stereo Review*
* *Yuppie Magazine*

Write to Celebrity Photos, Box 1335, Hanover, Massachusetts 02339.

335

Gifts for *him*: How about a hand-painted, personalized tie? In addition to custom ties made to your specifications, here are some of the personalized versions available from Chipp, Ltd.:

☞ A tie with *your* telephone number as the recurring design.
☞ A nautical flag tie, with signal flags spelling out your secret message.
☞ The "Stork Tie," with the name and birth-date of your new baby.

And, a catalog with hundreds of other stock designs is available. Included are ties illustrating career specialties, sports, hobbies, and 65 different breeds of dogs! Prices start around $24, with custom ties averaging $35. Call Chipp, Ltd., at 212-687-0850, or write or visit them at 11 East 44th Street, 2nd Floor, New York, New York 10017.

336

You *could* have a custom perfume created for your one-of-a-kind woman! Match the fragrance to her personality: Light and breezy, sophisticated and alluring, sexy and sensual.

☞ Helene Christina Perfumes, 241 Ensign Avenue, Beachwood, New Jersey 08722
☞ Caswell-Massey, 518 Lexington Avenue, New York City, New York 10017; 212-755-2254

Lame Excuses Department

337

Lame Excuse #1: "I don't have time."

Bullshit! You have 1,440 minutes every day—the same as everybody else. How you use those minutes is up to you. If she doesn't rank up there with your work, your ballgames, and your favorite TV show, why don't you simply get a dog for companionship and save yourself the trouble of dealing with another human being?

338

Lame Excuse #2: "I forgot."

That's okay. *Just don't do it again.* You're allowed to forget occasionally, but not consistently. If forgetting is a habit, you're sending a clear signal that she's just not that important to you. (If she's really *not* that important to you, why not be man enough to come right out and tell her, instead of making excuses?) See the chapter entitled "For the Forgetful."

339

**Lame Excuse #3 (Sub-category "Belligerent Excuses"):
"Real Men aren't romantic."**

Who the hell says so? Did you read it somewhere? Did your father tell you? Did you see it in a movie? What do you think? Never mind what *I* say—what do *you* think? What do you really think, believe and feel when you're alone and being completely honest with yourself? When you're not trying to impress your buddies; when you're not trying to bolster your self esteem.

If Real Men aren't romantic, then Real Men are *lonely*.

340

**Lame Excuse #4 (Sub-category "Whining and Complaining"):
"Being romantic is going to cost me a fortune!"**

As the Beatles said, "Money can't buy me love." It's true. Money can buy you companionship, attention, sex and status—but it can't buy you love or happiness. Being romantic *can* cost you a fortune, but it doesn't *have* to. Don't confuse the size of the sentiment with the size of the price tag. If you do, you're in for a rude awakening some day. (And any woman who only recognizes romantic gestures with a hefty price tag is really more interested in your checkbook than in you.)

341-344

Some strategies for overcoming Lame Excuses:

☞ Place a *standing order* with a friendly florist. Give him or her a list with all the important dates (birthday, anniversary, Valentine's Day), plus a few "just because" dates. Give him a price range. Give him your charge card number. Then, forget about it until the flowers start arriving automatically.

☞ Delegate more at work. Come home at a reasonable hour!

☞ Buy a book on time management. (Then make time to *read it.*)

☞ Analyze your priorities. Take an honest look at your entire life. Read some books, talk honestly with some friends . . . talk with *her!* Is she high enough on your list?

CLASSIC "LAME EXCUSES":

~

"REAL MEN AREN'T ROMANTIC."

"I'd like to, but I just don't have the time."

"Maybe next week."

"Being romantic is going to cost me a fortune!"

345

It's never too late to start anew. You can't *start over*—but you *can* start again.

Attitude Adjustment Section

346

Lower your inhibitions. Be spontaneous. Be silly. Be creative. Being a real romantic is a little like being slightly, enjoyably drunk. It lowers your inhibitions, causes you to act a bit silly sometimes, and gives you the impetus to act impetuous.

347

Want to keep your marriage (or long-term relationship) fresh and vital? *Live as lovers.* Remember that's how you started your relationship. You *can* recapture the glow, the passion and the excitement. It's largely a mindset, followed by a few active gestures. *Live as lovers.* Not just as husband and wife, mother and father, worker and housekeeper. First and foremost *you are lovers.*

In the Romance Class I've observed that in general, young people and others starting new relationships *start out* as lovers; and, many older couples have *re-discovered* that they are lovers. It's those intervening years that trip-up so many of us. *Live as lovers.* Write it down; repeat it to yourself; remind each other; leave messages on each other's answering machines.

348

Try being totally positive, accepting, supportive and non-judgmental for one entire week. No complaining, nagging, preaching, etc. It may change your life!

349

Make a list of all your past excuses for not being romantic.

☞ Repeat the following in a whiny voice: "I'm too busy." "I'm too tired." "I'm just not very creative." "Maybe next week." "I *want* to be romantic, but I'm just so forgetful." Now, repeat the following in a macho, belligerent tone: "Real Men aren't romantic!" "I have a career to think about!" "It's too expensive." "What the hell do you want from me, anyway?!" Good. Got it all out of your system? . . .

☞ Now, write your own list of excuses down on paper, put a big "X" through it, and give it to your lover with an attached invitation for a romantic dinner out.

350

For women: Stop nagging. Even if you're right. (*Especially* if you're right!) Hundreds of women in the Romance Class have verified the fact that nagging and complaining are the quickest ways to drive a man into a resentful, non-communicative—and far from romantic—silence.

351

For men: Stop judging. Stop correcting. Stop lecturing. She doesn't need it and she doesn't want it. You're not her father or teacher—you're her *lover*.

352

How to get a real bonehead to be romantic: You do something he *really* wants; then use it as a bargaining chip. [Hey, sometimes you just have to be ruthless!] Sometimes, to get his attitude changed, you have to change yours first. [Hey, nobody said life was fair!]

353

Do it without being asked. The un-asked-for gesture is most appreciated. The surprise gift is most cherished. And, when you take the initiative, you feel a sense of accomplishment. (You've also given your partner the best encouragement for responding in kind.)

A Kick-in-the-Pants

354

Do you take your partner for granted? *Well stop it!* Taking your partner for granted is not only the death of romance, but could well be the death of your relationship.

355

Take a risk—be romantic. *I dare you.*

Being truly romantic is a risky thing to do. I respect this difficulty and at the same time encourage you to leap off the cliff. Being truly romantic involves opening yourself up and revealing your feelings. Let's face it, nobody wants to be burned, and it's hard to risk a broken heart when you've been through a number of relationships.

- ❤ But if you're not going to open up to your lover, who else is there??
- ❤ And if you're consciously choosing *not* to open up, you might want to ask yourself what you're afraid of, or what you're hiding.
- ❤ And if you're not going to be romantic and open up, then what's the point of being in a relationship in the first place?!

356

Change one bad habit. Just *one!* (You'll be helping *yourself* as well as pleasing your partner!) Lose those 10 pounds you've been meaning to shed. Stop smoking. Eat more healthfully. Dress better. Exercise more. Listen better. Be more courteous. Slow your pace.

357

If it's your *partner* who needs a kick-in-the-pants, try this 3-part strategy:

1) Be more romantic to him. See if he responds in kind. Give it about two weeks to sink in. If he doesn't respond, then . . .

2) *Don't try to get him to be more romantic to you.* Instead, aim at changing his *level of awareness* about the need for more romance/intimacy/communication in your relationship. (Successful long-term changes in behavior usually follow a change in awareness. If you start with behavior modification, you'll probably only produce *short-term* results.) Some techniques for raising awareness include:
   - 🐵 Simply talking (heart-to-heart)
   - 🐵 Model romantic behavior ("Monkey see, monkey do!")
   - 🐵 Getting like-minded friends to set him straight
   - 🐵 Good psych/relationship books
   - 🐵 A class or seminar on love/romance/relationships
   - 🐵 Couple's counseling

   Failing all this, step three is . . .

3) Dump him. [Why should you put up with a relationship without spark and excitement?!]

358

Quit trying to do it perfectly. There's no such thing as The Perfect Relationship, and striving for one will only paralyze you. Once you eliminate the goal of perfection, nothing can hold you back! You'll lose your fear of "doing it right." You'll lose your fear of taking risks. And people who take risks, who live life creatively and spontaneously, tend to live more fun-filled, passionate lives.

359

Go out of your way for her. Being romantic only when it's convenient is like giving flowers on Valentine's Day—it's expected and it's no big deal!

360

Are you experiencing "Relationship Drift"? Has it been a *long time* since the two of you did something special/outrageous/romantic together? Has it been a long time since you talked heart-to-heart, made love, surprised one another? Wake up and smell the coffee! Don't forget that this person you're losing touch with was once your *lover.*

361

Go for it in a **BIG** way. Pull out *ALL* the stops. Don't TIPTOE into being more romantic. Be **Outrageous**lY romantic.

362

Decide to fall in love all over again. That's it—just *decide.* You don't need to read books that analyze your relationship. You don't need therapy. You just need to *decide.*

Just think of the great opportunity you have: The less romantic you've been, the more dramatic the change will be! I've had guys in the Romance Class simply *make up their minds* to be more romantic. They've reported that this simple decision led to their falling in love with their wives all over again. [Who am I to argue with success?!]

Sweet Stuff

363

Cheese Torte Royales—English Plum Pudding—Australian Dessert Apricots—"Razzberry Tart Bites"—Chocolate-Covered Blueberries!—Chocolate-Filled Peppermint Sticks—and *more* . . . from the Norm Thompson Catalog. Call 800-547-1160.

364

You know, of course, that green **m**&**m**'s are aphrodisiacs, don't you? With that as a start . . .

★ Present him with a bowl full of them.
★ Carefully open a one-pound bag of **m**&**m**'s and empty it out. Refill it entirely with green **m**&**m**'s. Seal it up so it looks like new. Give it to him for a snack.
★ Fill his box of Cheerios with green **m**&**m**'s.

365

Now, let's do a run of Hershey's Kisses ideas . . .

✳ Give her one.
✳ Give her one *thousand.*
✳ Remove all the little paper strips (that say "Kisses" on them) from a couple hundred Hershey's Kisses. Fill a little jewelry box with them. Wrap 'em up and present them to her.
✳ Write a clever certificate explaining that the little paper slips are coupons redeemable for one kiss each.

366

And then there are always "adult" candies and pastries! Check the ads in a local city magazine or look in the Yellow Pages under "Bakeries, obscene." The recipient must be a bit liberal, fun-loving and/or just plain dirty-minded. Chocolate body parts and suggestive cakes might be just the jolt your relationship needs. (Not recommended for first dates.)

367

What's her favorite kind of Girl Scout Cookie?

368

Think-up fun/clever/suggestive notes to attach to these candies: Good 'n Plenty, Mounds, Snickers, Almond Joy, Fire Balls, bubble gum, Life Savers or Hershey's Kisses.

Kid Stuff

369

Most women love stuffed animals.

370

Most men love gadgets, electronic stuff or tools . . . *"Boys' Toys."* Men never really grow up—our toys simply get more expensive.

371

Re-discover and nurture the "child" inside of you. It's the key to your creativity, sense of wonder and joy.

372

When's the last time you watched cloud formations? Take your lover for a walk in a field. Find an unobstructed view. Flop down on a hilltop. What do you see in the clouds? What do you imagine? [What *else* might you two be able to do together in the middle of a field??]

373

✦ Surprise her with a "Trinket Gift" hidden inside a Big Mac Container.
✦ Surprise him by hiding your favorite stuffed animal hidden inside his gym bag.

374

Get a favorite toy or item from his childhood: A toy, book, report card or picture from the wall. (Call his parents; they'll *love* to be a part of this idea.) Wrap it up and include a note.

375

Use your *own* kids' toys as tools. Crayons are great for writing short notes. Play-Doh is great for sculpting various body parts. (You probably won't want the children to witness this aspect of your creativity . . . "Mommy—what's *that thing?!*") Legos are great for spelling-out messages or leaving a trail through the house from the front door to your bedroom, where you're waiting for a little fun-and-games of your own . . .

376

Buy some crayons. If you're right-handed, take a crayon in your left hand. Write a short note to him as if you were in second grade.

377

Wind-up toys!—Monsters that walk and shoot sparks, creeping bugs, racing cars, crawling babies, lumbering robots, etc.!

vvvvvvvvvvvvvvvvvvvvvvvvvvvvvv

When a "me" and a "you" decide to become a couple, a new entity called "Us" comes into being.

~ GJPG

vvvvvvvvvvvvvvvvvvvvvvvvvvvvvv

378

Notes with stuffed animals . . .

- ✑ Teddy bears: *"I can't bear being away from you . . . "*
- ✑ Stuffed pigs: *"I'm hog wild over you!"*
- ✑ Stuffed lions: *"I'm roarin' to get you!"*
- ✑ Stuffed tigers: *"You're Grrrrrrreat!"*
- ✑ Stuffed monkeys: *"Let's monkey around . . . "*

379

Go fly a kite!

Funny Stuff

380

Send funny comics to him at work. Work-related. Hobby-related. Relationship-related. —He'll appreciate the fact that you thought about him.

381

(Is it true that most readers of *The New Yorker* buy it just for the cartoons?) *The New Yorker* is a *great* resource for relationship-oriented cartoons!

382

Get a favorite comic blown-up to poster size. (Head for your local copy shop.) Mount it on cardboard. Send it to her at work or prop it up on the front porch.

383

Re-write some comic captions; have them refer to the two of you.

384

➢ Tape a comic to the bathroom mirror . . .
➢ . . . or to the rear-view mirror in his car.
➢ Hide 20 comics all over the house.
➢ Insert them in dinner napkins.
➢ Stick them in cereal boxes.
➢ Attach them to the underside of the toilet seat.
➢ Fill his briefcase with them.

385

Get organized! Be prepared to send comics for years to come. Create a file or get a shoe box to hold your collection of comics.

386

Give him a book of collected comics. What's his favorite? The Far Side, Calvin and Hobbes, Peanuts, Cathy, Funky Winkerbean, For Better or For Worse, Blondie, Andy Capp, Pogo?

387

If your partner is a Pogo aficionado, the good news is that Walt Kelly's best cartoon books are once again available, after having been out of print for years. Choose from 10 hardcover classics, just $19.95 each (plus shipping). Call 800-GET-POGO, or write to Sunday Comics Store, 97 Sweet Briar Road, Stamford, Connecticut 06905.

- *Pogo Puce Stamp Catalog*
- *Pogo Sunday Book*
- *Deck Us All with Boston Charlie*
- *Beau Pogo*
- *We Have Met the Enemy and He Is Us*
- *Prehysterical Pogo*
- *The Return of Pogo*
- *Equal Time for Pogo*
- *Pogo's Sunday Punch*
- *Impollutable Pogo*

I'll be damned if I'll love just to love—
there's got to be more to it than that!

~ HUMPHREY BOGART

388

Funny stuff? You want *funny stuff!* Why didn't you say so? If you want *funny stuff,* you've got to check out The Lighter Side catalog. They've got piles of silly, funny, curious and otherwise odd things. Call 'em at 813-747-2356, or write to Post Office Box 25600, Bradenton, Florida 34206.

389

If your lover is a true comic fanatic, get him a subscription to *Editorial Humor.* It's a bi-weekly compilation of national and international cartoons. It combines the two best-read pages of the newspaper: The editorial page and the comic page. From your favorite funnies to political satire from Europe, it's all here. For more information call 617-666-2888, or Post Office Box 44-1289, Somerville, Massachusetts 02144.

Cool Stuff

390

✗ Wouldn't it be cool to take a Japanese flower arranging course?
✗ Wouldn't it be wild to rent a classic roadster for an afternoon?
✗ Wouldn't it be fun to stay in bed together all day on Sunday?

391

Place a full page ad in your local hometown newspaper to announce your anniversary, or celebrate his birthday, or simply to celebrate your love!

392

GIANT BANNERS are available from Supergram, by calling 800-3-BANNER. Overnight service is available for those *rush* occasions. The banners are printed on white or colored paper; lamination is optional; they're about a foot tall, and tend to run from 12 feet long to 30 feet or more, depending on your message. Here are some sample messages, lengths and costs:

I LOVE YOU—AND DON'T YOU FORGET IT (FOR A SECOND!)
(15 feet long, $9.95)

HAPPY ANNIVERSARY, AUGUST 25TH,
TO MY PEEPER, MY BUNNY-O,
MY WIFE!
(22 feet long, $13.55)

LET'S BE INDEPENDENT TOGETHER...
DON'T BE A FOOL... HEY, YOU!... "WAY!"... JE T'ADORE...
OOH-LA-LA!
(27 feet long, $15.95)

393

The Wireless catalog has all kinds of cool stuff in it. Garrison Keillor's Lake Wobegon stories on cassette tapes. Oddball books. Offbeat T-shirts. Classic radio tapes. And loads of great gift ideas. Wireless is the catalog for "fans and friends" of public radio, but I checked—and *anyone* can get it. Call 800-669-9999.

394

Present him with a "favor" (a gift bestowed as a token of goodwill; as a maiden's kerchief given to a knight)—something he'll carry around with him as a reminder of you.

✭ Classic: A kerchief or scarf
✭ Meaningful: A short verse printed on a ᴛɪɴʏ sheet of paper
✭ Intimate: Panties
✭ Silly: A little toy
✭ Personal: A lock of your hair

395

Wouldn't it be cool to *publish a book for her?!* If you can write at least 32 pages of prose or poetry, you can print-up a bookstore-quality paperback book for around $15 a book, for a minimum order of just 10 books! Graphic Illusions, on Cape Cod, loves to work one-on-one with people to help them produce their special books. [I've used them, so I can tell you from personal experience, that they're wonderful!] Graphic Illusions is *not* a "vanity press," but rather a quality printing operation that specializes in producing short-run books for personal or business use.

♥ You can supply camera-ready artwork and mechanicals.
♥ You can produce the artwork on computer via desktop publishing.
♥ You can hand them a disc, and they'll produce a book from it.
♥ Or, you can hand them a manuscript which they'll typeset, lay out, and then turn into a book!

Call them at 508-760-1321, or write to Post Office Box 99, Dennisport, Massachusetts 02639. (Turn-around time is usually just a few weeks!)

396

The coolest jigsaw puzzles I've ever seen are made by two companies that both have incredible catalogs. In addition to their regular puzzles, they'll create custom puzzles that you can use for all kinds of personal occasions. They've been used to spell-out wedding proposals, wish personalized birthday greetings, and help celebrate anniversaries.

- Stave Puzzles: 802-295-5200
- Bits & Pieces: 1-800-JIGSAWS

Love Is . . .

397

Love is . . . waking her gently with soft caresses and kisses.

398

Love is . . . eliminating all interruptions so you can *really* be alone together. Disconnect the phone; unplug the TV; ship the kids to the neighbors; disconnect the doorbell.

399

Love is . . . framing a favorite greeting card she's given you.

400

Love is . . . calling her from work to see if there's anything you can pick-up for her on your way home.

401

Love is . . . reading aloud to each other before bed.

402

Love is . . . being there to greet her at the airport—*regardless of what time her flight arrives or how inconvenient it is for you.*

403

Love is . . . having a poem delivered to your table at a restaurant.

404

Love is . . . sending her a postcard every day that you're away from her.

405

Love is . . . believing in one another.

Lovesongs

406

Lovesongs of the 1920s:

- ↠ L'Amour—Toujours—L'Amour
- ↠ I'll See You In My Dreams
- ↠ Ma—He's Making Eyes at Me
- ↠ Say It with Music
- ↠ Somebody Stole My Gal
- ↠ Who's Sorry Now?
- ↠ Indian Love Call
- ↠ Singin' in the Rain

- ↠ The Man I Love
- ↠ If You Were the Only Girl
- ↠ Someone to Watch Over Me
- ↠ Lover, Come Back to Me
- ↠ I'll Get By
- ♥ With a Song in My Heart
- ↠ Stardust

407

Stars
The
To

Lovesongs of the 1930s:

- ☞ What Is This Thing Called Love?
- ☞ Georgia On My Mind
- ☞ All of Me
- ☞ Dream a Little Dream of Me
- ☞ How Deep is the Ocean?
- ☞ Smoke Gets in Your Eyes
- ☞ Blue Moon
- ☞ The Very Thought of You

- ☆ Stairway
- ☞ I'm In the Mood for Love
- ☞ The Way You Look Tonight
- ☞ In the Still of the Night
- ☞ Falling in Love with Love
- ☞ All the Things You Are
- ☞ If I Didn't Care

408

Lovesongs of the 1940s:

✦ *You Stepped Out of a Dream*
☎ *Pennsylvania 6-5000*
✦ *A String of Pearls*
✦ *That Old Black Magic*
✦ *I Couldn't Sleep a Wink Last Night*
✦ *I'll Walk Alone*
✦ *I Love You for Sentimental Reasons*

✦ *If I Loved You*
✦ *Now Is the Hour*
✦ *Almost Like Being In Love*
✦ *A Fellow Needs a Girl*
✦ *On a Slow Boat to China*
✦ *Some Enchanted Evening*

409

Lovesongs of the 1950s:

✓ *La Vie en Rose*
✓ *The Little White Cloud That Cried*
✓ *Unforgettable*
✓ *Your Cheatin' Heart*
✓ *Secret Love*
✓ *You, You, You*
✓ *Love Is a Many-Splendored Thing*

✓ *If I Give My Heart To You*
✓ *Love Me Tender*
✓ *April Love*
✓ *Maria*
✓ *All I Have to Do Is Dream*
✓ *Put Your Head On My Shoulder*

410

Lovesongs of the 1960s:

➢ *Are You Lonesome To-Night*
➢ *Lay Lady Lay*
➢ *Moon River*
♥ *I Left My Heart in San Francisco*
➢ *As Long as He Needs Me*
➢ *More*
➢ *I Want to Hold Your Hand*

➢ *Baby Love*
➢ *Stop! In the Name of Love*
➢ *Strangers in the Night*
➢ *A Natural Woman*
➢ *Can't Take My Eyes Off You*
➢ *The Windmills of Your Mind*

411

Lovesongs of the 1970s:

❖ *We've Only Just Begun*
❖ *Ain't No Mountain High Enough*
✳ *Ain't No Sunshine*
✳ *You Are the Sunshine of My Life*
❖ *The Most Beautiful Girl*
❖ *Mandy*

❖ *Laughter in the Rain*
❖ *My Eyes Adored You*
❖ *Breaking Up Is Hard to Do*
❖ *I Like Dreamin'*
❖ *Three Times a Lady*
❖ *How Deep Is Your Love*

412

Lovesongs of the 1980s:

❦ *Endless Love*
❦ *Almost Paradise*
❦ *Against All Odds*
❦ *Didn't We Almost Have It All*
❦ *At This Moment*
❦ *Tonight I Celebrate My Love*
❦ *The Lady in Red*

❦ *Hold Me*
❦ *Somewhere Out There*
❦ *You and I*
❦ *Baby Come to Me*
❦ *Open Arms*
❦ *Never Gonna Let You Go*
❦ *Hard to Say I'm Sorry*

413

Lovesongs of the 1990s:

❖ *Don't Know Much*
❖ *All My Life*
❖ *Here and Now*
❖ *Right Here Waiting*
❖ *Wonderful Tonight*
❖ *Can You Feel The Love Tonight?*

❖ *I Will Always Love You*
❖ *How Am I Supposed to Live Without You*
❖ *Wind Beneath My Wings*
❖ *In Your Eyes*
❖ *Color Of The Wind*

414

Miscellaneous Rock 'n Roll Romance:

- ❦ *All My Loving*, The Beatles
- ❦ *And I Love Her*, The Beatles
- ❦ *Colour My World*, Chicago
- ❦ *Coming Around Again*, Carly Simon
- ❦ *Could It Be Magic*, Barry Manilow
- ❦ *Endless Love*, Diana Ross & Lionel Richie
- ❦ *Find One Hundred Ways*, Quincy Jones
- ❦ *Hearing Your Voice*, The Moody Blues
- ❦ *How Can I Tell You*, Cat Stevens
- ❦ *I Do, I Do, I Do*, Abba
- ❦ *I Need You*, America
- ❦ *I Should Have Known Better*, The Beatles
- ❦ *I Wish*, Stevie Wonder
- ❦ *I'll Never Leave You*, Harry Nilsson
- ❦ *I've Been Searching So Long*, Chicago
- ❦ *If I Fell*, The Beatles
- ❦ *If You Leave Me Now*, Chicago
- ❦ *In My World*, The Moody Blues
- ❦ *Just The Way You Are*, Billy Joel
- ❦ *Just You 'n Me*, Chicago
- ❦ *Knocks Me Off My Feet*, Stevie Wonder
- ❦ *Lend Your Love To Me Tonight*, Emerson, Lake & Palmer
- ❦ *Lessons Learned*, Dan Fogelberg
- ❦ *Looks Like We Made It*, Barry Manilow
- ❦ *Lost In Love*, Air Supply
- ❦ *Love Of My Life*, Abba
- ❦ *My Romance*, Carly Simon
- ❦ *Need Her Love*, Electric Light Orchestra
- ❦ *P.S. I Love You*, The Beatles
- ❦ *Rubylove*, Cat Stevens
- ❦ *Say You'll Be Mine*, Christopher Cross
- ❦ *She's Always a Woman*, Billy Joel
- ❦ *So Deep Within You*, The Moody Blues
- ❦ *So Far Away*, Carole King

414a

(More) miscellaneous Rock 'n Roll Romance:

- ❦ *Strange Magic*, Electric Light Orchestra
- ❦ *Summer Soft*, Stevie Wonder
- ❦ *The Right Thing to Do*, Carly Simon
- ❦ *Three Times A Lady*, Commodores
- ❦ *Until the Night*, Billy Joel
- ❦ *Weekend in New England*, Barry Manilow
- ❦ *Whenever You're Away from Me*, ELO & Olivia Newton John
- ❦ *Wishing You Were Here*, Chicago
- ❦ *Without You*, Harry Nilsson
- ✳ *You Are the Sunshine of My Life*, Stevie Wonder
- ❦ *You Make Lovin' Fun*, Fleetwood Mac
- ❦ *You Take My Breath Away*, Queen
- ❦ *You're My Home*, Billy Joel

I Love You

415

You could learn how to say "I love you" using sign language. These two books will show you the way:

- ✳ *The Joy of Signing*, by Lottie Riekoff
- ✳ *A Basic Course In American Sign Language*, by Tom Humphries, et al.

416

Love Stamps! Did you know that the U.S. Postal Service makes special "Love Stamps"? *Well, now you do!*—so you have no excuse! And, they issue a *new* Love Stamp every year. A yearly reminder to be more romantic from those incurable romantics in the federal government!

417

Upside down stamps on envelopes mean "I love you." (No, I didn't make this one up!! It's a tradition that was started during World War II, with soldiers and their lovers sending "secret love codes" to one another. This "code" caught-on in a big way, and continues to this day.)

418

"*I love you*"
(English)

"*Nagligivaget*"
(Eskimo)

"*Te amo*"
(Spanish)

"*S'agapo*"
(Greek)

"*Je t'aime*"
(French)

"*Aloha wau ia oe*"
(Hawaiian)

"*Ich liebe dich*"
(German)

"*Thaim in grabh leat*"
(Irish)

"*Ai shite imasu*"
(Japanese)

"*Ani ohev otakh*"
(Hebrew)

"*Ti amo*"
(Italian)

"*Jag alskar dig*"
(Swedish)

"*Wo ai nei*"
(Chinese)

"*Ya lyublyu tyebya*"
(Russian)

419

You can get your Valentine card postmarked from one of these romantic cities or towns:

- ♥ Valentine, Texas 79854
- ♥ Valentine, Nebraska 69201
- ♥ Loveland, Colorado 80537
- ♥ Loveland, Ohio 45140
- ♥ Loving, New Mexico 88256
- ♥ Bridal Veil, Oregon 97010
- ♥ Kissimmee, Florida 32741

Just put your card, complete with a stamp and address of your love, inside another envelope addressed to the Postmaster of the town of your choice. Attach a note requesting that your Valentine be hand-stamped and mailed. That's it!

I'm In the Mood for Love

420

☞ Send her an "invitation": Write that you're a researcher working on the new edition of *The Joy of Sex*, and you need her help with your studies.

☞ Send him an invitation: "Needed: An audience of one for an intimate Lingerie Fashion Show . . . "

421

Music sets the mood for love . . .

- ✳ Make custom tapes of romantic music.
- ✳ Find a good "Soft Jazz/New Age" radio station.
- ✳ Incorporate music into your day-to-day life together.

422

Albums for your Romantic Music Library:

➢ *She Describes Infinity*, by Scott Cossu
➢ *Openings*, by William Ellwood
➢ *Down To The Moon*, by Andreas Vollenweider
➢ *A Winter's Solstice*, by various Windham Hill artists
➢ *Childhood and Memory*, by William Ackerman
➢ *Out of Africa*, music from the motion picture
➢ *Barefoot Ballet*, by John Klemmer
➢ *Keys to Imagination; Optimystique; Out of Silence*, by Yanni

---

You sometimes work overtime at work, right?
Why not occasionally work "overtime"
on your relationship??

~ GJPG

423

Create special "signals" to let your lover know you're in the mood for love. Herewith, some ideas from creative Romance Class participants, and one or two ideas of my own . . .

♠ Have "Your Song" playing when he returns home from work.
♠ Play anything by Billie Holiday on the stereo.
♠ For men: Casually say, "I think I'll shave tonight . . . "
♠ One couple has "His" and "Hers" Japanese kimonos. The interested party changes into his or her robe . . . and if the other is interested too, he or she changes, also.
♠ One couple has a "family heirloom" pillow in their bedroom that says "TONIGHT" on one side, and "NOT TONIGHT" on the other side.

424

Some couples have created signals or gestures for use in *public,* all of which have essentially the same meaning . . .

☞ "I think I left the oven on. I'm afraid it's *getting hot . . .* "
☞ "Let's go home and watch TV."
☞ Hum "Your Song" in her ear.
☞ Scratch your left ear with your right hand.

425

For women: Put a red rose and a note on the lawnmower: "I appreciate the work you do. I'll demonstrate just how much I appreciate you when you're done with the lawn—but not a minute sooner!"

426

A variation on the theme . . . this one for men: Put a flower in the dishwasher or on the washer/dryer along with a note: "Have I told you lately how much I appreciate you? Why don't you meet me upstairs when you're done here. I'm warming-up a bottle of massage oil for you."

☆ Further variations: Pack the rose-and-note in his briefcase, in her suitcase, in the trunk of his car, or in her desk drawer.

427

Do you always make love at night? How about a little *afternoon delight?!*

428

Take an afternoon off work. See #427.

429

Don't leave lovemaking until just before sleeping! Why is it so often the last item on the list? [Why do so many people have their priorities so screwed-up?? How could those silly household chores possibly be more important than being intimate with your lover?]

430

Recognize, capitalize on, and compensate for the physiological differences between men and women that affect lovemaking:

➤ Following "the act," most men want to roll over and go to sleep . . . while most women are wide awake and crave more intimacy. What to do? Well, you guys could realize that the chemical that makes you feel sleepy is effective for only a few minutes. If you can just wait-it-out, you'll feel awake and revitalized again!

➤ Did you know that most men's hormone level is highest in the morning, while most women's is highest—you guessed it—in the evening?! [What a dirty trick!] It's just a fact of life. Compensate. Take turns. Be understanding.

431

Go in search of her G-Spot. You may not find it, but you'll have a great time looking! (You may want to pick up a copy of *The G Spot*, by Alice Kahn Ladas, et al.)

432

Drip honey on various parts of your lover's body. Lick it off. (Wine and cordials work nicely, too.)

Words of Love

433

❝*I love you.*❞ The all-purpose, over-used phrase . . . that we never tire of hearing. (When's the last time you told her?)

434

Memorize her favorite poem, or the lyrics to her favorite love song. Recite it at private times, or while making love.

435

☞ Write-down the words to her favorite poem or lovesong, then mail it to her.
☞ Write it on elegant parchment paper. Use a fountain pen.
☞ Have it rendered in beautiful calligraphy.
☞ Frame it!

436

Words of love from *The Prophet:*

> *Love one another*
>> *but make not a bond of love.*
> *Let it rather be a moving sea*
>> *between the shores of your souls.*

~ Kahlil Gibran

437

Some classic words of love . . .

Shall I compare thee to a summer's day?
Thou art more lovely and more temperate:
Rough winds do shake the darling buds of May,
And summer's lease hath all too short a date:
Sometime too hot the eye of heaven shines,
And often is his gold complexion dimm'd;
And every fair from fair sometime declines,
By chance, or nature's changing course untrimm'd;
But thy eternal summer shall not fade,
Nor lose possession of that fair thou ow'st,
Nor shall death brag thou wander'st in his shade,
When in eternal lines to time thou grow'st;
 So long as men can breathe, or eyes can see,
 So long lives this, and this gives life to thee.

~ Sonnet 18, by William Shakespeare

438

Words of love from the best-selling book of all time . . .

Love is patient, Love is kind,
 it does not envy; it does not boast; it is not proud.
It is not rude, it is not self-seeking,
 it is not easily angered, it keeps no record of wrongs.
Love does not delight in evil
 but rejoices with the truth.
It always protects, always trusts,
 always hopes, always perseveres.

~ I Corinthians 13:4-7

439

Words of love . . . words of commitment . . .

When I give my heart away, you know that it's forever;
As I give my love I give my Word to you.
And as our lives unfold for us, we'll watch them bloom together,
Every moment we shall see the world anew.

Who can say why love has brought us here,
   who can say where love will lead?
It's enough to know that love will show the way.
And the Vow we take to love, in both our fullness and our need,
Will be ever living as it is today.

So here we stand together, and here we make a stand,
To offer love to Holiness, in faith to understand . . .
That if living is for loving, and if only Truth is true,
Then I dedicate myself to loving you.

As love roots out the obstacles, and brings them up to see,
We shall offer them to Truth and let them go . . .
Like a forgotten song remembered, with the words and melody,
Love arises from within to take us Home.

So here we stand together, and here we make a stand,
To offer love to Holiness, in faith to understand . . .
That if living is for loving, and if only Truth is true,
Then I dedicate myself to loving you.

~ BRIT LAY
"WEDDING SONG"
ILLUSIONS AND DREAMS
(SEE #534)

440

Familiar words of love . . .

> *How do I love thee? Let me count the ways.*
> *I love thee to the depth and breadth and height*
> *My soul can reach, when feeling out of sight*
> *For the ends of Being and ideal Grace*
> *I love thee to the level of everyday's*
> *Most quiet need, by sun and candle-light.*
> *I love thee freely, as men strive for Right;*
> *I love thee purely, as they turn from Praise.*
> *I love thee with the passion put to use*
> *In my old griefs, and with my childhood's faith.*
> *I love thee with a love I seemed to lose*
> *With my lost saints,—I love thee with the breath,*
> *Smiles, tears, of all my life!—and, if God choose,*
> *I shall but love thee better after death.*

~ Elizabeth Barrett Browning

441

This item is a surprise gift for my wife. [You get the record—and the rest of the verses—when you discover this item.]

> *I can take all the madness the world has to give*
> *But I won't last a day without you.*

~ Paul Williams
"I Won't Last A Day Without You,"
Life Goes On

442

Do you think you're the only one who writes "mushy," exuberant poetry?
Think again . . .

Miss you, miss you, miss you;
Everything I do
Echoes with the laughter
And the voice of You.
You're on every corner,
Every turn and twist,
Every old familiar spot
Whispers how you're missed.

Oh, I miss you, miss you!
God! I miss you, Girl!
There's a strange, sad silence
'Mid the busy whirl,
Just as tho' the ordinary
Daily things I do
Wait with me, expectant
For a word from You.

~ David Cory, selections from *Miss You*

443

Classic words of love . . .

She walks in Beauty, like the night
Of cloudless climes and starry skies;
And all that's best of dark and bright
Meet in her aspect and her eyes:
Thus mellow'd to that tender light
Which heaven to gaudy day denies.

~ Lord Byron, first stanza of *She Walks In Beauty*

444

Words of love (short and sweet):

I love you,
Not only for what you are,
But for what I am
When I am with you.

~ Roy Croft, first stanza of *Love*

445

Revive the lost art of writing love letters!

446

Do you feel silly trying to write a *love letter?* Do you think it's not cool to express your true/passionate/insecure feelings? Maybe you'd feel more comfortable if you could only see someone *else's* love letters, huh?

Here are selections from some love letters that may give you encouragement (and perhaps some ideas):

⊠ A letter from Napoleon Bonaparte to Josephine De Beauharnais:

> *"I wake filled with thoughts of you. Your portrait and the intoxicating evening which we spent yesterday have left my senses in turmoil. Sweet, incomparable Josephine, what a strange effect you have on my heart!"*

⊠ A letter from King Henry VIII to Anne Boleyn:

> *"I beseech you now with all my heart definitely to let me know your whole mind as to the love between us; for necessity compels me to plague for a reply, having been for more than a year now struck by the dart of love . . ."*

⊠ A letter from John Keats to Fanny Brawne:

> *"Sweetest Fanny, you fear, sometimes, I do not love you so much as you wish? My dear Girl I love you ever and ever and without reserve. The more I have known you the more have I lov'd . . . The last of your kisses was ever the sweetest; the last smile the brightest; the last movement the gracefullest . . ."*

⊠ A whole *bookful* of passionate outpourings is available in *Love Letters,* edited by Antonia Fraser.

447-449

Choose one of these assignments. Complete it in the next week.

☞ *"Why I love you."* Make it into a scroll. Give it to her with a red ribbon tied around it.

☞ *"I remember when we first met . . ."* Write it in the style of a romance novel or in another literary style that you prefer.

☞ *"Ten reasons why I married you."* Have it rendered in calligraphy and have it framed.

Myths of Romance

450

A *major* myth: The *very concept* of a "Battle of the Sexes."

Ridiculous! There's no such thing. It's media hype—a good way to get on a TV talk show. There's no "Battle of the Sexes"—*jeesh!* The very thought is ludicrous. Now, there *are* "gaps" that separate us: A few physiological differences [*Vive la différence!*], and some definite psychological ones. But nothing worth terming a "battle." (A thought: Even if there *were* such a thing as a "Battle of the Sexes," and your side actually *won*—just *what* would you be winning?!)

451

Another myth that affects romance: "Nice guys finish last."

That's one of the most idiotic-yet-widespread untruths ever sold to adolescent boys in American culture. No wonder European men often sweep women off their feet with Old World style, grace and romance.

452

Three widespread myths about romance:

Being romantic will . . .

1. *Save your relationship.*
2. *Improve your sex life.*
3. *Cover-up your faults.*

No, no, no! Romance will *not* accomplish any of these things. Romance is about *expressing love*—it's not a guarantee that you'll live happily ever after. Will romance improve your sex life? Well, a little bit, perhaps. But if you've got heavy, deep-seated issues, romance is *not* the answer. And romance certainly won't cover-up your faults! Romantic gestures may disguise your faults in the short-run—but your true personality will always reveal itself. Having realistic expectations about romance will enhance your enjoyment of it.

453

What *will* romance do for you?

Romance will enhance the quality of your life.

Romance will take your relationship from whatever level it's functioning at, and "bump it up" a level—to a place of more fun, more spontaneity, more passion and intimacy. (Sounds like a good deal to *me!*)

454

Another myth promulgated in the men's locker room: "Give her an inch and she'll take a mile."

If you "give an inch" on a consistent basis, you'll satisfy any woman. It's when you're stingy with those romantic gestures that a woman builds up so much resentment that she demands "a mile" from you. And rightfully so.

455

A myth that women tend to believe:

➤ "I can change him."

> ➤ You can't "change him"—if by that, you're referring to his "Core Personality Traits." There are some things that you just can't change about people! (You can't turn a night owl into a morning person; you can't turn a homebody into an outdoorsman—don't try!)

> ➤ But you *can* affect his "Peripheral Personality Traits." (You can get him to be more aware of your needs; you can help him remember anniversaries; you can encourage more communication.)

Do you have 20 years of experience—
or one year of experience repeated 20 times?

~ GJPG

456

Another "women's myth":

➤ "He's hopeless!"

> ➤ Nobody's *totally* hopeless. Be patient; be loving; be creative. And don't forget that there are some good and valid reasons why you're with him . . . Do you remember what they are? (Does *he* remember what they are? Maybe you can help him remember . . . and re-ignite the passion that once was there.)

> ➤ The thousands of diverse men who've benefited from the Romance Class are living proof that it's not hopeless!

457

Myth-Buster #1: "One 'scores points' for making romantic gestures." ("This dozen roses should be good for at least three back rubs!")

458

Myth-Buster #2: "Planning kills spontaneity." (This one belongs in the "Lame Excuses Department.")

Rituals of Romance

459

Rit'-u-al, noun. **1.** an established ceremony that recognizes the specialness of something (an idea or person). **2.** observance of regular practices that hold special meaning for the participants.

Create your own "Rituals of Romance"! This American culture of ours is sadly lacking in rituals and ceremonies. With the passing of many ethnic cultural traditions that used to hold people and families together, it's time we started *creating our own*!

460

Rituals can be elaborate, serious and meaningful. Or they can be fun, silly and quirky. They can be personal, private and secret, or public and shared.

461

➤ Write a toast, just for the two of you. Use it whenever having wine.
➤ Variation on a theme: Write *two* toasts: One for private use, and one for public use.

462

One couple in the Romance Class told us that they celebrate a ritual "Monthly Calendar-Changing" ceremony. They're both gardeners and nature lovers, and they have a beautiful flower calendar in their living room. On the first of every month, they ceremoniously pour two glasses of brandy, change the calendar to a new month, and toast each other and the passage of time.

463

Another couple celebrates the changing of the seasons by taking a walk together on the first day of Summer, Autumn, Winter and Spring *regardless* of what the weather is like.

464

One husband has created a "ritual" phrase with which he introduces his wife: " . . . And I'd like you to meet my *bride*, Alice." (Alice, his 64-year-old wife of 40 years, always blushes.)

465

Sit down once a year, write a short poem for your lover, have it rendered in beautiful *calligraphy*, frame it and present it. It could become a tradition that fills entire walls with framed sentiments.

466

Some couples have *morning* rituals:

✶ They spend 10 minutes talking in bed before rising.
✶ They read an affirmation aloud to one another.
✶ They make a point of kissing before parting.

467

Some couples have *evening* rituals:

➢ They go for a walk after dinner together.
➢ They meditate silently together.
➢ They take turns every other night giving each other backrubs.

468

And, there are Sunday morning rituals:

♠ Attending a church service together.
♠ Reading the Sunday Funnies aloud to each other.
♠ Sunday brunch.

469

My wife and I have a little "car ritual" we've performed for as long as we've known each other: I always unlock the car door for her (regardless of which one of us is driving), and she always leans over and unlocks my door from the inside. I never really thought of it as a "ritual" until recently; it's just a little thing we *always* do that helps us not take the other for granted.

470

One man brings his girlfriend a cup of tea before bed every night—*whether she wants one or not.*

"It's very sensitive of you to realize that men <u>like</u> to get flowers!"

471

One woman came to her marriage with a vast collection of very special Christmas tree ornaments. Her husband jumped on the bandwagon, and they now have a ritual "Search for This Year's Special Ornament."

Do's and Don'ts

472

Don't buy a dozen roses on Valentine's Day. It's common, it's expected, and it's expensive. (Economics 101 teaches: "Prices rise when demand rises." Horticulture 101 adds: "You couldn't possibly pick a more difficult time than mid-February to demand that roses be ready to bloom in North America." Therefore, costs go up, and so do prices. Don't blame your local florist!!)

✳ Instead, buy a Bonsai tree for her.
✳ Or choose flowers that match her eyes.
✳ Or pick a bouquet of wildflowers.
✳ (All right, all *right* . . . If you feel you simply *must* buy roses, get one beautiful, fresh red rose. No pink, yellow or white for Valentine's Day!)

473-474

☞ *Don't* buy gifts at the last minute. (Economics 101 warns: "Desperate shoppers never find what they want, and they always pay top dollar for it. Desperate buyer beware!")

☞ *Do* plan ahead. (Romance 101 teaches: "Plan ahead, and you'll never be at the mercy of opportunistic retailers.")

475

Don't buy practical items for gifts. Appliances are wonderful, but *don't give them as gifts!* [My father-in-law learned this lesson the hard way. For their very first Christmas together, he gave his wife . . . an electric broom. To put it mildly, she was not pleased.]

476

Exceptions to the previous item:

- ❑ Gourmet kitchen utensils (for the fanatical chef).
- ❑ Tools (for some men).

My informal poll of Romance Class participants indicates that only 2% of the women would enjoy practical gifts, while about 60% of the men would appreciate practical items.

477

✓ *Don't* give cash as a gift—unless it's done creatively.

- ✫ Tape lots of one dollar bills together, creating a long banner out of them, and wind them around the Christmas tree, or string them throughout the house.
- ✫ If his favorite color is green, tie a stack of one dollar bills with a green ribbon.
- ✫ Attach a hundred dollar bill to a Victoria's Secret catalog, along with a note saying, "You choose."

✓ *Don't* give checks as gifts.

478

Don't give gift certificates. They're generally too generic.

- ✦ **Exception #1, for women:** A generous gift certificate for her all-time favorite store.
- ✦ **Exception #2, for men:** A gift certificate from Sears or Radio Shack or The Sharper Image.
- ✦ **Exception #3, for both:** *Custom-made* gift certificates that express your affection in a special/creative/unique or touching way.

479

Contrary to popular belief, you should *not* use romance to apologize after a fight! If you do, you'll taint *all* your romantic gestures for a long time to come. (After a fight, a simple, sincere apology is best. Resume romantic gestures *after* you've both cooled down, or after a week—whichever is later.)

480

Know your anniversaries. *All* of them . . .

* Your wedding
* The day you first met
* Your first date
* Your first kiss
* Your first . . .

* The first time you made love
* Your first big blow-out fight
* The day you moved-in together
* The day you bought your home
* The first time you said "I love you"

Note: Some people feel that the only important anniversary is their wedding date. That's fine! They feel that other dates just clutter things up. And then there are people who like to celebrate *every possible significant date they can think of.* That's fine, too. (The danger is when each of you adheres to the opposite philosophy. And in this case, opposites usually attract . . . just like the Universal Law of Opposites #2, which states that "Women who love to dance always marry men who hate to dance.")

481

Don't relate to your lover as a stereotype. He's an individual, not a statistic. And she's a unique person, not "just like all women."

Today's tabloid topics, talk-show trends, and sex surveys have only limited relevance to you and your lover and your relationship. Take it all with a large grain of salt. *You'll never lose by treating your partner as a unique and special person.*

Fun and Games

482

Do a *Cosmo* quiz together.

483

Go to a carnival, fair, or amusement park together. (Without the kids.) Plan to blow an entire roll of quarters on silly games.

484

Visit the New England Carousel Museum! On display are more than 300 animals—from horses to hippocampi (sea monsters with the forelegs of a horse and the tail of a fish). The museum, located in Bristol, Connecticut, is open year-round. Call 203-585-5411.

485

Ladies, fulfill a fantasy: Arrange a surprise ski weekend; give him a backrub; greet him at the door in high heels and garter belt.

486

Guys, fulfill a fantasy: Run a bubble bath for her; cook dinner; rent her favorite movie; make love *the way she wants to be made love to.*

487

Check your local Yellow Pages, under "Costumes: Masquerade and Theatrical." And then . . .

* Rent a costume, surprise her! Be a cowboy, doctor, policeman, mechanic, cave man, astronaut.
* Rent a costume, surprise *him*! Be a ballerina, policewoman, doctor, girl scout, classy callgirl, elf.

488

Go on a "Toy Store Shopping Spree." Each of you takes 10 dollars, and buys toys for yourself. Take them home, unwrap them, and tell your partner why you bought what you bought. You'll learn a lot about each other.

489

Go on a mall-wide "Trinket Gift Hunt." Here's how it works: You each get 10 dollars and 30 minutes to shop for each other. The goal is to buy as many different fun/crazy/significant/silly "Trinket Gifts" as possible, for your partner. Meet back in the center of the mall, open your gifts, and be prepared for a hilarious time!

The quietly brave, the creatively intimate,
the gently strong—they are
the lovers, the peace-makers,
the saviors of the world.

~ GJPG

Weird and Wacky

490

Greet him at the door with confetti.

491

Practice "Telepathy Romance." When you're going to be apart, agree to stop whatever else you're doing and *think about each other and nothing else for one minute*, at a pre-determined time.

492

Practice "Leap Year Romance." When February 29th rolls around, take the day off work and declare it your own personal "Romance Day." [Hey, why should your *employer* get that extra day??—especially if you're on salary! Give the gift of time—24 hours worth—to your lover!]

493

Giftwrap a wishbone in a jewelry box. Send it to her with a note that says, "I wish you were here."

494

Is your partner crazy over cribbage? (Apparently there are *millions* of cribbage fanatics out there . . .) Sign him up in the American Cribbage Congress. You'll stay informed of all the regional and national tournaments. Write to Box 5584, Madison, Wisconsin 53705.

495

Is he a *Doctor Who* fan? Sign him up to be a member of The Companions of Dr. Who. Write to P.O. Box 56764, New Orleans, Louisiana 70156.

496

Have you ever seen $10,000 in one dollar bills strewn about someone's living room? Well, neither have I—but one woman in the Romance Class reported that that's what her husband did with a commission check he received one year after a big sale. He handed her a rake and said, "Honey, whatever you can fit into this garbage bag is yours to spend!" (Being rather clever herself, she stacked the bills *neatly* and walked away with *all of it!)*

497

Speaking of money... Did you know that you can write a check on *anything?* As long as you include all the important numbers on the item, it's legal, and the bank will cash it!

- One guy presented his wife with a check written on a mattress!
- Another wrote a check on a pair of panties.

498

Kidnap her! Blindfold her; drive her around town until she's definitely lost; then reveal your destination: Her favorite restaurant, or maybe a romantic inn!

Odds and Ends

499

Add flair to your love notes with festive, wacky or personalized rubber stamps from Ink-A-Dink-A-Do! They have *thousands* of different stamps:

- 💐 Hearts ❤ and stars ☆ and moons ☾ and initials and symbols
- 💐 Bears and butterflies and birds and beetles and bows
- 💐 Musical notes and Holiday Greetings and snowflakes
- 💐 And personalized name-stamps
- 💐 And totally custom-created stamps ☞ ☞ ☞
- 💐 And stamps made from photos

For just two bucks you can get a very cool, very fun catalog. Write to Ink-A-Dink-A-Do, Department 1001, 60 Cummings Park, Woburn, Massachusetts 01801; or call 617-938-6100; or visit their cart at the Faneuil Hall Marketplace in Boston.

500

When he's returning from a trip, decorate your front lawn, front door, trees, bushes and porch with streamers, banners, signs and balloons. [Why should you care if the neighbors think you're nuts?!?]

501

- ★ Men: Go through her *Cosmo* or *Ladies Home Journal, Time, McCall's, Self, Glamour* or *New Woman* magazine and write funny comments in the margins, circle significant articles or headlines, and give your opinion on some of the ads.

- ★ Women: Same with his *Sports Illustrated, Esquire, GQ, New Yorker, People* or *Playboy* magazines.

502-504

Ideas for cat lovers!

✻ "Eine Kleine Kat" and 18 more "Songs of the Cat" are featured on this wonderful recording that celebrates our feline friends. Radio humorist Garrison Keillor and international opera star Frederica von Stade join conductor Philip Brunelle for an hour of superbly entertaining selections. $10.95 for the cassette; $13.95 for the CD. Call the Wireless Catalog at 800-669-9999.

✻ Two magazines for friends of felines:

   ✳ *Cat Fancy Magazine.* Call 714-855-8822, or write Fancy Publications, P.O. Box 6050, Mission Viejo, California 92690.
   ✳ *Cats Magazine.* Call 904-788-2770, or write P.O. Box 290037, Port Orange, Florida 32129.

✻ There is a cat museum in Amsterdam, Holland! Called the Cat Cabinet, it features works of art highlighting the role of the cat in art and society. For more info call the Netherlands Board of Tourism at 312-819-0300, or write to them at 225 North Michigan Avenue, Suite 326, Chicago, Illinois 60601.

505-506

Ideas for dog lovers!

➤ Visit the Dog Museum, in its handsome new quarters near St. Louis. The museum is devoted to the collection, preservation and exhibition of works of art and literature related to Man's Best Friend. The museum is in the Trot Jarville House, a magnificent Greek Revival building in Queeny Park, 25 miles west of downtown St. Louis. Call 314-821-3647.

➤ Two magazines for dog lovers:

   ✳ *Dog World Magazine.* Call 312-726-2802, or write 29 North Wacker Drive, Chicago, Illinois 60606.
   ✳ *Dog Fancy Magazine.* Call 714-855-8822, or write Fancy Publications, Inc., P.O. Box 6050, Mission Viejo, California 92690.

507

And for lovers of other popular pets . . . there's *Bird Talk Magazine* and *Aquarium Fish Magazine*, from those animal lovers at Fancy Publications. Call 714-855-8822, or write P.O. Box 6050, Mission Viejo, California 92690.

Mindset of a Romantic

508

Romantics are flexible.

★ Decide on the spur-of-the-moment to take a half day off work!
★ Consciously "change gears" at the end of the day—from your "business mode" into your "personal mode." Most working people need to practice turning their feelings back on at the end of the day.

509

Romantics are mind-readers.

Yes, being more romantic enhances your ESP! Actually, those who are tuned-in to their lovers—those who listen well—develop a kind of "sixth sense" about what their lovers would love. One of the best things about long-term relationships is that you develop this sense. And as it develops, your relationship deepens and your intimacy grows.

★ Get her a *gift*—not a *present*. (See #16)
★ What has he *really wanted* for a long time, but held back from buying? Get it for him!

510

Romantics have a good sense of humor.

There's no such thing as a "humorless romantic." While the *foundation* of romance is a serious love, the *nature* of romance is lighthearted.

☆ Do you laugh together a lot?

☆ Do you let your True Self shine through? (Or are you playing a role? Favorite roles include The Responsible Provider, The Good Mother, The Big Shot Executive, The Long-Suffering Spouse.—Loosen up, for crying out loud!)

☆ Do something ZaNy tonight.

511

Romantics are passionate (#1).

I'm not talking about sexual passion here, but about a passion for *life*. Romantics don't allow their lives, or love lives, to slide into boredom—the deadly enemy of all relationships.

★ Express the true depth of your feelings for your lover.

★ What is your *lover* passionate about? Recognize it, act on it.

512

Romantics are passionate (#2).

Yes, as a matter of fact, romantics *do* tend to be more sexually passionate than the average mortal. (Just another of the many side-benefits of the romantic lifestyle!)

513

Romantics "work at it"—and "play at it," too!

Being a romantic is not the same as being a starry-eyed, unrealistic dreamer. Romantics often work long and hard to pull off some of their "romantic masterpieces." Romantics plan and scheme, buy gifts ahead-of-time, search for sales, and stock-up on greeting cards.

And, of course, romantics play and have a lot of fun. If you haven't gathered that by now, there's probably no hope for you.

514

Romantics are always "dating."

Familiarity breeds contempt *only if you let it!* There are *thousands* of ways to keep your relationship fresh and new.

➤ "Courtship After Marriage" is an apt phrase coined by famous motivational speaker Zig Ziglar. (It's also the title of an excellent book he wrote. Check it out!)

➤ Many long-term couples in the Romance Class have "date nights" on a weekly basis.

515

Romantics live in the moment.

"Carpe diem"—*seize the day!* Don't put it off until tomorrow! Do something passionate for your lover. Do it now! Do it with feeling!

✳ Do something unexpected for your lover *today!*
✳ Do something totally outrageous.
✳ Do something totally out of character for you—surprise her!
✳ Do something sexy.
✳ Do something sensitive.
✳ Do something creative.

516

*Romantics are **magnets** for romantic ideas.*

Romantics find romantic ideas *everywhere.* They read the newspaper not only for the news, but for romantic opportunities. [Heck, I consistently get great romantic ideas from *The Wall Street Journal.* There was the article on how to spend less time at work (and more time at home) by utilizing technology wisely. And then there was the ad for the company that makes customized chocolate bars for corporate clients—or for lovers!]

* Romantics have a portion of their brains assigned to the task of recognizing romantic opportunities when they appear. Other people screen them out.
* Romantics notice unique gifts when shopping for other things.

517

Romantics are cheerleaders.

Romantics are the biggest fans of their lovers. They provide enthusiastic support, constant encouragement and unconditional love. (They don't succeed 100% of the time, naturally, but they're always in there trying.)

→ Have you complimented her lately?
→ Have you thanked him recently?

518

Romantics are creative.

They see their relationships as opportunities to express their creativity, as arenas for self-expression, as safe havens for experimenting, and as places for growth.

✐ *Write* something: A love letter, a love note, a little poem, a silly song, or just a line!
✐ Create your own quirky "Love Coupons." (See #918)

519

Romantics have their priorities straight.

What are your *true* priorities? Where do you really expend your time, energy and creativity? Rank these categories according to their relative importance in your life: Relationship-Family-Faith-Health-Work-Community-Education-Leisure. How do your priorities line-up?

★ Say to her, "Let's plan a special outing: A lunch-date, dinner-date, movie—whatever. You choose the time and place, and I'll be there—*regardless of my previous plans.*" This shows that she has top priority—over work, friends, hobbies, etc.

★ You sometimes work overtime at work, right? Why not occasionally work "overtime" on your relationship??

The Gospel According to Godek

520

Romantic gestures have no ulterior motive. Their only purpose is to express love and appreciation; to show that you've been thinking of your partner. (This is a goal to strive for, one that we rarely achieve perfectly. That's okay. Don't worry about it. Just keep moving forward.)

521

Men and women are much more alike than we are different. We tend to have different *styles,* but we all have the same *needs.* Be *aware* of the differences, but don't *exaggerate* them. In fact, why don't you *celebrate* them? *Romance, properly used, can be a bridge between the sexes.*

522

☞ Romance is an art, not a science: You can't predict it or "get it" perfectly. So you logical, "left-brained" folks are going to have to loosen up, let go and get creative!

☞ Romance is not a sport. It's not a competition: No points are awarded.

☞ Romance is not a business. There's no bottom line.

523

Romance is a state of mind, an attitude. It's not so much *what* you do as *how you do it.* This is why little gestures work so well. It's also why some people (mostly men) just don't "get it" when it comes to romance. If you approach romance and relationships with a cynical attitude—or a rigid, overly-practical state of mind—you just won't tune-in to what's going on here.

524

Romance doesn't equal love. It's the *expression* of love; the language of love; the real-world expression of an ideal.

525

Employing the concept of "Couple-Thinking" will automatically turn anyone into a romantic. Couple-Thinking is a technique in which you *first* think of yourself as a member of a couple, and second as an independent individual. (Men, and our culture in general, put too much emphasis on rugged individualism, and not enough emphasis on relationship-building and connection-making.) [Note: I am *NOT* suggesting that you martyr yourself on the altar of Relationships.]

526

❤ The highest form of romance is *optional romance*—gestures made that are not required or expected.

♥ The middle form—*obligatory romance*—is that which is required by custom or culture. It's important, but of minor consequence in the larger scheme of keeping relationships functioning at a high level of passion.

♨ The lowest form—*reluctant romance*—is hardly worth mentioning. It's dishonest on the part of the giver, and an insult to the recipient.

527

Beware of the phenomenon of "Relationship Entropy"—the tendency of relationships to become more diffuse if not cared-for and nurtured; the tendency for once-close lovers to drift apart if both of them don't work at it on a consistent basis. [File under "Better Relationships Through Physics Concepts."]

My Personal Favorites

528

The Perpetual Bouquet™—invented by my wife, Tracey, during the writing of this book! She started bringing me one flower a day, and placed it in a vase on my desk. After a few days, I had a complete bouquet. She continued this for *several weeks*—removing one old flower and replacing it with a new one—so I had an ever-changing, always-fresh reminder of her love and support for me.

529

One of *my* rituals is a changing-of-the-seasons ceremony which uses framed covers from *New Yorker* magazines. We have four covers for each season that hang in our living room. Each season we put on appropriate music, change the covers, and toast each other with Baileys Irish Cream or B&B Liqueur.

* ❉ We celebrate *five* seasons: Winter, Spring, Summer, Autumn and Christmas.
* ❉ Favorite music includes George Winston's albums: *Autumn, Winter Into Spring,* and *December.*

530

I'm fascinated by Bonsai trees . . . so my wife (then girlfriend) surprised me by sending me to a Bonsai class at Bonsai West, a local shop specializing in the art of miniature trees. It was truly a *gift.* The Bonsai-lovers at Bonsai West not only grow and create the tiny, elegant trees, they've also figured out how to ship them safely anywhere in the country! Call them at 508-486-3556.

531

Last year I substituted my wife's regular Christmas stocking with *real silk stockings*. (Santa was delighted to fill them with goodies!)

532

A honeymoon discovery: "Angel Bells," also known as "Tinker Bells," sometimes known as "Tranquility Balls." They're little spheres (half-inch, one-inch or two in diameter) made of sterling silver that have the most pleasant-sounding soft chimes inside them. My wife and I each have one that we carry occasionally as a reminder of each other. They tend to be found in unique jewelry shops, cool/gifty boutiques, and in some gift catalogs.

533

My favorite romantic songs:

✦ *Something*, The Beatles
✦ *In The Mood*, Glenn Miller
✦ *I Won't Last a Day Without You*, Paul Williams
✦ *You Are So Beautiful (To Me)*, Joe Cocker
✦ *Lessons Learned*, Dan Fogelberg
✦ *One Summer Dream*, Electric Light Orchestra
✦ *Closer To Believing*, Emerson, Lake & Palmer
✦ *Just The Way You Are*, Billy Joel
❤ *Coming Around Again*, Carly Simon
✦ *Watching and Waiting*, The Moody Blues
✦ *You've Got a Friend*, James Taylor
✦ *Wedding Song*, Brit Lay (See next item)

534

✦ Well on its way to becoming a Wedding Classic, a new song called "Wedding Song" was the selection we chose for our wedding ceremony. This wonderful, touching song is from the cassette tape *Illusions and Dreams,* a collection of uplifting and spiritual songs by singer/composer/guitarist Brit Lay. (Another great lovesong from the tape is "By Myself.") You, too, can have *Illusions and Dreams* (on cassette) for just $12.50, by writing to Box 127, Barnstable, Massachusetts 02630. (See #439 for the complete lyrics to "Wedding Song.")

✦ New! Brit's second album, *Heart-To-Heart,* has recently been released. Mellow, thought-provoking, happy music! Just $12.95 for the cassette, and $15.50 for the CD.

535

I invented *The LifeChart*™ to celebrate my wife's birthday last year. I drew a timeline representing her life—from birth to the present. Along the line are noted events from her life: Significant, outrageous, funny and serious. (I interviewed her parents and friends for items that I had no way of knowing.) Parallel timelines indicate a few events from my life, and some world events, for putting her life into perspective. It became an instant heirloom. (And for our tenth anniversary, in the year 2000 . . . the *updated* version!)

536

The Victorian Inn. Small, elegant, quiet. In Edgartown on Martha's Vineyard Island, just off Cape Cod, Massachusetts. Your gracious hosts, Karen and Stephen: 508-627-4784.

Satin and Lace

537

Ladies: If you remember only *one thing* from this book, remember this: Men *love* lingerie. Hundreds of men in the Romance Class have confided or complained that having their ladies wear more lingerie is the one thing they want intensely that their women tend to hold back on. (Scan through a *Playboy* or *Penthouse* magazine. You'll discover that *there are very few naked women in them.* They're almost always wearing stockings, garter belts, or lacy/frilly little things.) Take note. Take action.

538

For those of you who are a bit timid about walking into a lingerie shop, here's help from a few catalogs:

~ *Victoria's Secret Catalog—800-888-8200*
~ *Playboy Catalog—800-423-9494*
~ *Frederick's of Hollywood Catalog—800-323-9525*

539

I conducted a little *more* research on your behalf, and here's what I found:

~ *Dream Dresser—800-963-7326*
~ *Barely Nothings—800-4-BARELY*
~ *Maitresse—800-456-8464*
~ *Fashion Fantasies—800-858-0565*

540

Gentlemen: Approach the subject *gently*.

❑ Your first lingerie present should *not* be a peek-a-boo bra.
❑ You might start by giving her a say in the matter: Attach a hundred dollar bill to a lingerie catalog along with a note saying "You choose." Or custom-make a "Lingerie Coupon."

541

In addition to their usual clothing, Victoria's Secret boutiques also carry "Long Stem Panties." They're like roses, only . . .

542

Why not mail a lingerie gift to her—*at work*.

[Picture this: She opens her mail about 11 a.m.; she gets your package. After she recovers and regains her composure, she's totally distracted for the rest of the day. Sounds good to me!]

543

Use your imagination: Create your own "Panty-of-the-Month Club"!

544

Men: Many lingerie shops hold regular "Men's Nights"—complete with refreshments and a fashion show.

Le Boudoir

545

The bedroom is your *private, romantic hideaway*. Don't turn it into an all-purpose room.

* Get rid of that TV!
* No bright lights!
* No exercise equipment.

* Keep flowers on the nightstand.
* Always have candles handy.
* Massage oil is a must.

546

Don't simply have breakfast in bed—make it an elegant feast. Use your good china and crystal. Add candles and flowers.

547

"Breakfast in bed is 'nice'—but rather *common*, don't you think?" said one couple in the Romance Class. "We think the class would be interested in one of our favorite pastimes: *Dinner* in bed!"

548

The True Test of Love & Tolerance #1:

Let her warm her cold feet on you in bed.

549

Voted "Most Romantic Types of Beds":

* Canopy beds
* Brass beds

550

☞ Leave a rose on her pillow.
☞ Leave a note on his pillow.
☞ Lay-out the lingerie outfit you'd like her to wear.
☞ String little white Christmas tree lights around the window frames.
☞ Spread rose petals all over the bedroom.

551

From my informal, ongoing poll of Romance Class participants: "Most Romantic Positions (. . . for *Sleeping*)"—from most to least romantic:

   1st: "Pretzel"   2nd : "Spoons"   3rd : "Bookends"

For Men Only

552

Read the book *You Just Don't Understand—Women and Men in Conversation*, by Deborah Tannen, Ph.D. It offers revolutionary insights into the difficulties men and women have communicating with one another. As the book's intro says, it offers " . . . a totally new approach to a peace treaty in the battle between the sexes."

553

Pick up a copy of *Cosmo* or *Glamour* or *Self* or *Savvy* or *New Woman* or *Family Circle* or *Ms. Magazine* or *Ladies Home Journal*. [How do you expect to know what women are thinking about and talking about if you don't peek at their magazines occasionally?]

554

A shopping trip for men. Buy one item from each store. Giftwrap in separate boxes and give!

- ✔ A bath shop
- ✔ A lingerie boutique
- ✔ A local card shop
- ✔ A local liquor store
- ✔ A neighborhood flower shop
- ✔ A quality jewelry store

555

Another shopping trip for men (product-specific):

Pick-up all these items in coordinated fragrances (Apricot, Garden Delight, Spring Rain, etc.): Body lotion, hand lotion, shampoo, conditioner, foaming bath gel, perfumed soap, fragrance candle, dusting powder and potpourri. She'll love you for it. Guaranteed.

556

* A word to the wise: *Don't equate romance with sex.* It's one of the quickest ways to foster resentment and miscommunication. Equating the two tends to turn romance into barter.

* A corollary: Romance sometimes—*but not always*—leads to sex. Romance is *always* about love, but only *sometimes* about sex. Got it?!

557

Be *extra* nice to her during her menstrual periods. (Mark the dates on your calendar as a reminder!)

558

❦ Do a household chore that's usually one of "her" jobs:
- ☞ Cook dinner
- ☞ Clean the bathroom
- ☞ Do the grocery shopping
- ☞ Take the kids to baseball practice

❦ Now, combine this with one of the ideas in the "Bubblebaths" chapter, and she'll *really* flip!

559

If you want your lover to wear lingerie more often, *why do you think that you have the right to slouch around in your ratty boxer shorts or dirty sweat pants?!* Take a hint! Get a nice bathrobe, or silk pajamas, or a lounging jacket, or a Japanese kimono!

560

Shave on Saturday night.

561

Do you treat your employees better than you treat the woman in your life? A lot of men do. [What *is it* with you guys?!] Here's a hypothetical role-playing exercise for you: View your lover as a customer, client, or employee. Good managers think of ways to motivate their employees, they don't simply order them around or take them for granted. And salesmen are always considerate of their customers . . . After all, customers are very important. Well, isn't she just as important?! Think about it! *Get your priorities straight!*

562

Do something *with* her that you hate to do (and do it cheerfully without complaint): Go dress shopping with her; go out to a movie with her; attend the ballet with her; do some gardening with her.

563

Do something *for* her that you hate doing: Go grocery shopping, wash the dishes, weed the garden, get up in the middle of the night with the baby.

Time and effort expended are usually more appreciated than money spent.

~ GJPG

564

Buy her an *entire* outfit. Include: Beautiful lingerie, a gorgeous dress, a matching scarf, pin or necklace, and shoes! Spread 'em out on the bed. Wait for her jaw to drop.

565

Listen to her! Don't problem-solve; don't give advice; don't agree or disagree. Just *listen.* Validate her.

Often, when men think women are looking for *answers,* they're simply looking for *compassion and understanding!* (This is one of those sex-based differences: Men tend to be oriented around problem-solving; women around relationships.)

For Women Only

566

Send him a letter sealed with a kiss. (Use your reddest lipstick.)

567

Send him a *perfumed* love letter.

568

Send him flowers at work.

569

Greet him at the door wearing sexy lingerie! Or your high school cheerleader outfit. Or a fantasy costume. Or . . . !

570

Don't position yourself against his passions. Don't force him to choose between you and his golf/football/basketball/cars/fishing! As they say, "If you can't beat 'em, join 'em!" Read a book about his favorite sport/hobby/ pastime so you can join in, or at least understand what's going on.

571

Do something *with* him that you hate to do (and do it cheerfully and without complaint). Go fishing, bowling, bird-watching, running or camping with him; watch "The Game" on TV.

572

Many men would consider this the *Ultimate Gift:* A "Fantasy Photo" of you. You can get a sensual, provocative and stunning "Fantasy Portrait" made of yourself by contacting a photographer who specializes in the growing art form often called "Boudoir Photography." Many of these photographers are women with a talent for making their subjects feel comfortable, and then bringing out the subtle, sexy side of your personality, and capturing it on film. "Lingerie" portraits seem to be most popular, followed by "Fantasy Outfit" shots and nude photography. Check the Yellow Pages under "Photographers," or look in the classified ad section of your local city magazine, or call one of these photographers:

❧ Lucienne Photography, New York City: 212-564-9670

❧ Fantasy Photography by Daphne, Arlington, Massachusetts: 617-641-2100

573

Take a quick look through *Playboy* or *Penthouse*—see for yourself what men find sexy. Ask him what he likes and doesn't like. (You might be surprised at what you learn about him! You might also open up the door to more frank discussions about sexuality and sensuality.)

574

Read the book *Iron John*, by Robert Bly. It offers a fresh and insightful look at masculinity. Learn that the "Wild Man" inside him need not turn him into an insensitive macho guy; see the partnership that the book offers between the masculine and the feminine. (If your man hasn't already read this book, give it to him when you're finished with it.)

575

Do something *for* him that you hate doing. Iron his shirts; wash his car; cook his favorite, hard-to-make dinner; run some errands; cut the lawn.

For Singles Only

576

Mail her a copy of your business resumé instead of a greeting card. Attach a note: "I'd like you to get to know me better." (Other stuff to send: A grammar school report card. A photo of yourself as a baby.)

577

Listen for "Pings" in your relationship. Just what are Pings?? They're any action or habit your partner has that you *just know you couldn't live with for the rest of your life.* For example:

§ You're in the car, scanning radio stations for some classical music. You cringe when you hear "Stayin' Alive," but she squeals "Oh, I *love* the Bee Gees!" *(Ping!)*

§ He told you to prepare for a "special night out" because he's got "box seat tickets." Expecting to attend the symphony and dine at the Posh Cafe, you spend hours getting ready, and dress in your classiest outfit. He shows up in jeans with two tickets to the Red Sox game. *(Ping!!)*

Note: One person's Ping may be another person's cherished quirk. Pings are relative things!

578

I don't know about *you* guys, but when I was single and in a relationship, I always had cause to celebrate once a month—or once every 28 days, to be exact. Why not celebrate the onset of her menstruation with a little champagne? For you, it can be a celebration of relief; and for *her*, it might ease the discomfort a bit.

579

Romantic Strategy #1 for Cleverly Meeting Someone At Work: Send a dozen pink roses to her anonymously; then place one pink rose on your desk, where she's sure to notice it. (You take it from there . . .)

580

So now you've got 1001 ways to be romantic . . . You *still* need someone to be romantic *with!* Finding the Right Person is obviously an important part of the equation. Would you like a little professional help in your search? According to many of the single participants in my Romance Classes, the best of the many services is **Together Introduction Service.** They match people based on compatibility, and they've matched over *half a million* people in the last 21 years! **Together** has offices in more than 175 cities worldwide. Look 'em up in the Yellow Pages and get a head start in your search for love!

581

You've been dating a while, you're considering "getting serious," but you're not sure that he's really everything you're looking for. How do you evaluate the relationship? With this simple formula:

70% + spark = A-OK

In other words, if this person has at least 70% of the qualities you want your ideal partner to have, plus you have "spark" (passion and romance; you're soul-mates; you "click")—go for it! You *know* you're not going to get 100% (there ain't no Prince Charming!)—but you'd better not settle for less than 50%!

582

Guys: When giving jewelry, never, never, *never* package it in a ring box, unless . . . it's an engagement ring. You're probably totally unaware of it, but those little square boxes spell one thing to women: M-A-R-R-I-A-G-E. Ask the jeweler to give you a different kind of box, or present the piece in a creative, crazy way. Why ask for trouble?

583

✢ If you've talked about maybe moving in together, and you decide you want to go for it, place your apartment key in a gift box, wrap it up and give it to her.

✢ Or—mail it to her with a note: "You've got the key to my heart . . . now I want you to have *this* key."

For Marrieds Only

584

✭ In the middle of a party or other social event, turn to her and whisper, "You're the *best.*"

✭ Turn to her in public and whisper, "I'm glad I married you."

585

❦ Re-frame your wedding invitation. Hang it on the wall.

❦ Have your wedding vows penned in beautiful *calligraphy.*

586

"Re-frame" your relationship:

✳ She's not your wife—she's your *lover.*

✳ He's not your husband—he's that handsome devil that you fell head-over-heels in love with, remember?!

587

✳ Frame your wedding license and hang it on the wall.
✳ Send him a copy of your wedding license; attach a note: "Do you remember when?"

588

Guys: On your wedding anniversary, re-create her wedding bouquet. [If this doesn't bring tears to her eyes, divorce her.] Since you probably don't know a chrysanthemum from poison ivy, show one of your wedding photos to your florist.

589

Dig out your wedding album. Have a new 8-by-10-inch print made of the best photo of your bride. Wrap it up and give it to *yourself* for your birthday or for Christmas.

□□□□□□□□□□□□□□□□□

To have and to hold, from this day forward,
For better or for worse, for richer or for poorer,
In sickness and in health, to love and to cherish,
Till death do us part.

~ BOOK OF COMMON PRAYER

□□□□□□□□□□□□□□□□□

590

Carry a copy of your wedding license in your wallet, next to your driver's license.

591

➤ Go on a second honeymoon.
➤ Go on a *third* honeymoon.
➤ Re-enact your first date.
➤ Re-stage your wedding.

592

Regardless of how long you've been married, start referring to your wife as "My Bride."

593

Save your "Just Married" sign (or make a new one). Tape it to the back windshield of your car before taking a Sunday afternoon drive. People will honk and wave . . . you'll feel like a newlywed again!

594

Re-visit the place where you proposed marriage. Take along a bottle of champagne. Reminisce!

595

✦ Renew your wedding vows. Create a *private* ceremony. (Make it special, unique and meaningful to the two of you. Use music from back when you first got married, combined with your favorite music from the years since then. Gather meaningful symbols and cherished gifts to create an altar.)

✦ Renew your wedding vows in a *public* ceremony. Declare your love in front of all your friends. Party!

596

I posed this rhetorical question in the first edition of *1001 Ways To Be Romantic*, which listed the traditional and modern gifts for wedding anniversaries: "Just *who* made up this list, anyway??" No one has been able to answer the question, so I figure *my list* is just as good as anybody else's!

Year	Traditional	Modern	Godek's
1	Paper	Clocks	Lingerie
2	Cotton	China	Flowers
3	Leather	Crystal/glass	Lingerie
4	Fruit/flowers	Appliances	Software
5	Wood	Silver/silverware	Books
6	Candy/iron	Wood	Lingerie
7	Wood/copper	Desksets	Wine
8	Bronze/pottery	Linens/laces	Cameras
9	Pottery/willow	Leather	CDs
10	Tin/aluminum	Diamond jewelry	Jewelry
11	Steel	Fashion jewelry	Silk
12	Silk/linen	Pearls	Perfume
13	Lace	Textiles/furs	Umbrellas
14	Ivory	Gold jewelry	Lingerie
15	Crystal	Watches	Computers
20	China	Platinum	Champagne
25	Silver	Silver	Jacuzzis
30	Pearl	Diamond/pearl	Canoes
35	Coral	Jade	Sculpture
40	Ruby	Ruby	Stocks & bonds
45	Sapphire	Sapphire	Lingerie
50	Gold	Gold	Rolls Royce
55	Emerald	Emerald	Gold
60	Diamond	Diamond	Vacations

597

Some books you oughta look up:

* *Why Did I Marry You, Anyway?* by Arlene Modica Matthews
* *Dave Barry's Guide to Marriage and/or Sex*
* *The Oxford Book of Marriage*, edited by Helge Rubinstein

Married . . . With Children

598

Send your kids to summer camp. It just might revitalize your marriage unlike any specific romantic gesture *ever* could!

599

Instead of having the babysitter come in while you go out, *have the babysitter take the kids out—while you two stay home!* Send all of them to a movie—a *double feature.* ("Now, what was it we used to do with all this peace and quiet? *Oh, yes . . . !*")

600

Hang a "DO NOT DISTURB" sign on your bedroom door when you want a little privacy. Enforce this directive strictly! (For your toddlers: Teach them to read "Do not disturb" before "Once upon a time.")

601

Guys: Add Mother's Day to your list of *Obligatory Romance* dates to observe. Mark it on your calendar *now*.

"WHY DO YA WANT TO BE ROMANTIC?
YOU'RE **ALREADY** MARRIED!"

602

Guys: Give your *wife* a gift on your kids' birthdays. (Why should the kids get all the gifts? Your wife is the one who did all the work!)

603

Make special "Love Coupons" to help each other deal with the kids:

✯ An "I'll get up in the middle of the night with the baby" coupon.
✯ An "It's my turn to stay home with the next sick kid" coupon.
✯ A coupon for "Five 'taxi trips': Hauling the kids to soccer practice."
✯ An "I'll cook the kids' dinner" coupon.

604

The old "Distraction Diversion": Rent several of their favorite movies ("E.T.," "Star Wars," "The Little Mermaid," "Friday the 13th, Part VII"); buy a 10-pound bag of popcorn. The kids sit hypnotically in front of the TV while the two of you escape upstairs.

605

Create a neighborhood "Child-Sharing Program." Arrange entire weekends when one family on the block plays host to "The World's Biggest Slumber Party," while the rest of you get romantic.

Engaging Ideas

606

Apply for the job of "Husband"!

☞ Write an "Engagement Resumé" outlining your desirable qualities, your qualifications and relevant experience. Write an appropriate cover letter, and mail it to her or present it in person.
☞ You may want to send a copy to her parents! [Then again, maybe not!]

607

One man in the Romance Class was inspired to present his girlfriend with one red rose . . . which had a diamond ring hidden inside the unopened bud. The rose sat on her desk for two days, where she admired it and smelled it often, before it bloomed, revealing the ring!

608

Some engaging ideas from Romance Class participants:

☞ "Romantic" hiding places for diamond rings: Inside boxes of Cracker Jacks [what a prize!], among flowers, at the bottom of champagne glasses, tied to balloons.

☞ "Romantic" locations for proposals [Don't forget that *your* definition of what's romantic doesn't necessarily apply to everyone!]: Baseball stands, classy restaurants, fast food restaurants, in bed, in elevators, in the place where you first met, in subway cars, over the phone, on cassette tape, at the beach, on vacation . . .

609

Here are some of the more creative and unusual ways that other people have gotten engaged:

- ✭ Skywriting proposals
- ✭ Sky banner proposals
- ✭ Custom jigsaw puzzle proposals
- ✭ Videotaped proposals
- ✭ Proposals on billboards
- ✭ Proposals inside custom made Chinese fortune cookies
- ✭ Audiotaped proposals
- ✭ Telegrammed proposals
- ✭ Using lit candles to spell-out "Will you marry me?"
- ✭ Painting the proposal on the roof, then taking her flying!

610

Some couples consult astrologers for the best dates and times to get engaged. Others choose their wedding dates based on the stars. [Hey, why take chances?]

611

Ladies: Make a photocopy of your hand and new engagement ring. Attach a note saying "I've got a piece of the rock." Mail it to him.

612

Men: A touch of class: Send a clever telegram to her parents, asking their permission to marry their daughter.

613

Engagement Rings for Men™! Why should women be the only ones to get engagement rings??

○ From a woman's point-of-view: Engagement rings are public statements that you're "spoken for" or "taken." Why should *he* be running around "free"?

○ From a man's point-of-view: You just dropped several thousand dollars on a diamond—and you get *nothing?!*

[A report from the "Practice What You Preach Department": Yes, my wife gave me an engagement ring. In fact, I have *three* rings. They're three coordinating bands that symbolize Love, Peace and Happiness.]

614

Plan ahead . . . *way* ahead! Get a friend to buy 50 of the top magazines and newspapers that are on the newsstand on your wedding day. Pack them safely away, and present them to your partner on your 25th wedding anniversary!

Generating Ideas

615

Set a goal of generating or discovering one new romantic idea each day for a year. Your commitment will help draw ideas to you. You won't have to work hard at this, I promise!

616

Look through today's newspaper for romantic ideas. A trained eye will spot something romantic nearly every day. Sometimes it will be in an ad; other times it will be in articles, on the Op-Ed page, or on the comics page.

617

Once you find these romantic gems, you've got to *save them*! File them or fill a shoebox with them or stash them under your bed—anything that works for you, as long as you can dig them out later. [This book is essentially a compilation of years and *years* of collected stuff, together with my thoughts, observations and insights—all written down on scraps of paper, and eventually included in the Romance Class.]

618

Institute the "Buddy System." Team-up with a good friend and act as each other's personal "Romance Coach." Encourage each other, trade ideas, remind each other of important dates, compare notes and share new discoveries.

619

"Tune-in" to romantic ideas. It's like tuning in to a radio station. Romantic ideas are being broadcast all the time!

- ❦ Here are some "stations" for you to tune into: Stores, window displays, billboards, newspapers, magazines, ads, articles, friends and acquaintances, bookstores, card shops and catalogs.
- ❦ Assign a small portion of your brain the task of being constantly on the look-out for romantic ideas. Write yourself notes for two weeks to get you into the habit. (Put them on the car dashboard, in your appointment calendar, on the bathroom mirror, on a clock face.) The goal is to re-train your mind to stop filtering-out those ideas, and start letting them seep in.

To be loving is to be creative.
To be creative is to express love.

~ GJPG

620

"Hang out" in a variety of stores: Card shops, stationery stores, lingerie departments, trendy gift shops, music stores, her favorite store, his favorite store, magazine stands and bookstores. You don't have to go often—just occasionally. Just drop in and hang out every once in a while. Why? To find out what's new! To spark your creativity! It helps if you put yourself into environments that foster a romantic attitude.

621

Hold a "Romantic Idea Brainstorming Session" with a group of friends.

✶ Serve pizza and beer. Hand out pads of paper and markers. Use a large pad on an easel to compile ideas.

✶ The goal is to generate *as many ideas as possible* in one hour. Serious and silly; practical and unrealistic; expensive and cheap and free; thoughtful and outrageous; suggestive—and outright obscene; meaningful or not; complicated or simple; gifts or presents; gestures, places to go and things to do!

622

Skim through the Yellow Pages for 20 minutes or so. Jot down some interesting-sounding companies that might offer potentially romantic products or services. You'll be amazed at what you'll discover.

623

Practice creating "Variations On A Theme" for generating romantic ideas. Start with any idea and "build on it," expand it, extend it.

❋ Start with "greeting cards": Buy one; buy 100! Make some yourself. Send one-a-day for a week, send one-a-day for a month! Frame some cards that she's given you.

❋ Start with "candy": What's her favorite? Buy tons of it. Fill her shoes with candy; fill her purse, her glove compartment, her pillow. Send it to her at work. Spell out words with it. Create trails throughout the house with it.

624

Keep your *partner's* likes/passions/hobbies in mind. What is her favorite color, author, poet, artist, movie, TV show, song, singer, wine, perfume, restaurant, ice cream, sport or flower? (See the chapter called "Memorize This List!"—pages 219 to 221.)

625

Tap into the strength of your personal style and your special talents. Do you have a flair for writing, dancing, building things, organizing, cooking or drawing? Use these talents and abilities to enhance the romance in your life!

➤ Sit down and literally take an inventory of your own personal talents, interests, skills, aptitudes, passions, etc. Write a list. Keep it handy. Use it as an idea-generator.

626

Lots of romantic ideas will appear if you focus on your partner's "Orientation." An Orientation isn't really a hobby—it's more an intense interest or generalized passion. It's something that tends to occupy his mind, time and interest. (Someone who is really "into" his Irish heritage isn't exactly practicing a *hobby*, but his "Irishness" is a great focus for you when thinking-up romantic ideas for him.) Don't ever compete with his Orientations—participate in them! Here are a variety of Orientations expressed by Romance Class participants:

☞ Cats	❊ Shopping	➤ WW II
☞ Dogs	❊ Specific sports	➤ Ethnic heritage
☞ Region of country	❊ Specific actors	➤ Puzzles
☞ Hometown	❊ Clothes!	➤ Golf
☞ College	❊ Music, classical	➤ Science fiction
☞ Comics	❊ Music, specific type	➤ Do-it-yourself
☞ Lingerie	❊ Music, specific artist	➤ Food!

Getting to Know You

627

Interview his mother, father, siblings, friends and colleagues—to learn about his unique quirks, likes, dislikes, hobbies and passions.

628

"Fantasy Window Shopping." Pretend you're millionaires; window shop together and choose items for yourself as well as gifts for your partner. Keep it light. Dream. Fantasize! Later, over dinner, talk about *why* you chose various items. You'll learn a lot about each other.

629

❋ What's the difference between "sexy" and "sleazy"? What's the difference between "cute" and "coy"?—I'll bet your definitions differ from one another's. An open discussion won't be easy, but it will certainly be eye-opening! And important.

❋ Skim through *Playboy* or *Penthouse* magazine together. Learn what he thinks is sexy.

❋ Skim through her favorite romantic novel. Learn what she finds sexy.

630

☆ Play "Show and Tell": Pick a beloved object. Talk about its history and why you like it. (An old baseball glove; a doll from childhood; something given to you by a grandparent; a stuffed animal; a trophy; a piece of jewelry, etc.)

☆ A variation: Visit places that have special meaning to you.

631

Write a "Personal Resumé." Imagine that you're applying for a job as her boyfriend or husband—or his girlfriend or wife. What kind of resumé would you prepare? Write it up in the standard business resumé format— but be creative with the content! (This idea is fun for singles, and surprisingly educational for long-time marrieds. Try it!)

632

Have your astrological charts analyzed by an expert. Have a "reading" done together. Record it on cassette tape for review later. You'll learn a lot—and have fun—regardless of whether you're a believer or a skeptic. (See the chapter called "Starstruck" for one of the best astrologers on the East Coast.)

633

Have your handwriting analyzed! The art and science of graphology has come a long way, and you'll be amazed at what can be "read" in your writing.

Making Beautiful Music Together

634

Create a custom tape of meaningful/romantic lovesongs for her—songs with great romantic lyrics.

* Choose about 10 great songs, and record them on a cassette tape.
* Don't just *hand* the darn thing to her—give it to her in a Walkman, or insert it in her car tape player with a little note attached!

635

Mood music! If you want the music, but you'd rather not have someone else singing pretty words into her ears while you're trying to nibble on them, there's lots of instrumental music available. From the comfortable, jazzy sounds of Chuck Mangione, to the floating, gentle piano solos of George Winston, you can find something to fit your mood. Or, you can *create* the mood with the music. The classical/jazz compositions of Jean-Pierre Rampal and Claude Bolling will help create a lovely, light-hearted mood; while Johann Pachelbel's *Canon in D* will definitely create a peaceful, thoughtful mood.

Love is the harmony of two souls singing together.

~ GJPG

636

Some specific albums to add to your Romantic Music Library:

★ Chuck Mangione: *Feels So Good; Main Squeeze; Chase the Clouds Away*
★ Dan Fogelberg & Tim Weisberg: *Twin Sons of Different Mothers*
★ George Benson: *Livin' Inside Your Love; Breezin'*
★ George Winston: *Autumn; Winter Into Spring*
★ John Klemmer: *Touch; Lifestyle (Living & Loving)*
★ Jean-Pierre Rampal & Claude Bolling: *Suite for Flute & Jazz Piano*
★ Johann Pachelbel: *Canon in D (The Pachelbel Canon)*

637

Create a custom music tape of romantic instrumental music—*background* music. This kind of music is great for creating the right environment for candlelit dinners or romantic lovemaking sessions.

638

Submitted for your consideration:

- ❦ *And I Love Her,* The Beatles
- ❦ *Colour My World,* Chicago
- ❦ *Endless Love,* Diana Ross & Lionel Richie
- ❦ *Find One Hundred Ways,* Stevie Wonder
- ❦ *Hearing Your Voice,* The Moody Blues
- ❦ *Just The Way You Are,* Billy Joel
- ❦ *Lessons Learned,* Dan Fogelberg
- ❦ *She's Always a Woman,* Billy Joel
- ❦ *The Most Beautiful Girl In The World,* Frank Sinatra
- ❦ *Unforgettable,* Nat King Cole
- ❦ *I Wanna Be Loved By You,* Marilyn Monroe

639

The "Thompson Vocal Eliminator" can remove virtually all of a lead vocal from a stereo record, cassette or CD—and leave the background! A great gift for the "Secret Sinatra" or "Madonna Wanna-Be" in your life! Write for a free brochure and demo record: LT Sound, 7980 LT Parkway, Lithonia, Georgia 30058; or call 404-482-4724.

Communicating

640

Listen, for a change. You'll learn a lot about your partner.

- ➻ Listen for the feelings behind the words. We don't always say what we mean, but the emotional content is still there if we tune-in to it.
- ➻ Listen without interrupting. (Quite a challenge—especially if you've been together for many years!)

641

Respond with love, *regardless* of what your partner says or does. Why? Because behaviors such as complaining, worrying, shouting and nagging are all *disguised calls for love*. (When a child exhibits these kinds of behaviors we instinctively understand that it comes from fear, and has nothing to do with us personally. Unfortunately, we rarely grant adults this courtesy.) Try to respond to what's *really* going on, not simply to what's on the surface.

642

Give your partner more reassurance. Reinforce her good qualities. Compliment his talents and abilities. Reinforce all the good qualities *that attracted you to your partner in the first place.*

✧ Tell him what you really appreciate about him.
✧ Remind her that you really do adore her.
✧ Concentrate on the positive when talking to him.
✧ Focus on who she *really is*, instead of on your unrealistic fantasy of "The Perfect Woman."

643

One woman in the Romance Class told us that she and her husband of 40 years have a phrase for a special mode of communication that they strive to practice as much as possible. They call it "Courtship Conversation." Here are the guidelines for Courtship Conversation:

✶ Talk to one another *with respect.*
✶ Remember that conversation involves *two-way* communication.
✶ No judging, assuming or second-guessing the other person.
✶ Complete honesty is demanded, assumed, and never questioned.
✶ Speak from the heart, but don't leave the head behind.
✶ Maintain eye contact.
✶ Practice with each other at least one hour a day.

644

* Learn to read the subtle signals, the non-verbal clues, the body language and tone of voice that your lover uses.

* Pay attention to the "codes" your partner uses automatically and unconsciously. For example, here's a list of behaviors that was generated in one of the Romance Classes:

  * Talking non-stop
  * Withdrawing
  * Criticizing unfairly
  * Shouting
  * Nagging

All of these *different* answers were responses to the *same* question! I'd asked the class how their partners act when they're stressed-out about work. Different people use different "codes." The better you get at de-coding your partner's behavior, the stronger your relationship will be.

645

Be aware that *men and women tend to have different styles of communicating.* Deborah Tannen, author of *You Just Don't Understand,* says that a man engages the world as "an individual in a hierarchical world social order in which he [is] either one-up or one-down." A woman, on the other hand, approaches the world as "an individual in the world of connections. In this world, conversations are negotiations for closeness in which people try to seek and give confirmation and support, and to reach consensus."

646

Be aware of the differences in men's and women's styles of communicating, *but don't over-emphasize them.* If you focus on the gap, you'll overlook the bridges!

➤ Bridge #1: The fact that underneath all our differences in style, men and women all want the same things: To be loved, cared for, respected and appreciated; to have a place of safety and security, where we can be ourselves, grow, experiment and mature.

➤ Bridge #2: Romance itself. Romance is a bridge between the sexes, as it is the expression of love. Romance is a language that uses words, gestures and tokens to communicate the subtle, multi-faceted and complicated feelings of love.

Togetherness

647

Read the Sunday newspaper in bed together.

648

✗ Go bicycling together.
✗ Rent a bicycle built for two!

649

Invite her to accompany you on your next business trip. (All work and no play makes hubby a bore.)

650

Explore together: Auctions, flea markets, second-hand stores, garage sales and rummage sales. They're great places to find "Trinket Gifts" as well as practical stuff you just might need around the house.

Drawing by Lorenz © 1985 The New Yorker Magazine, Inc.

"So I'm not Leo Buscaglia, but I'm not Attila the Hun, either."

651

Buy a Leo Buscaglia *videotape!* Watch it together.

   ✯ *Speaking of Love*   ✯ *A Time to Live*   ✯ *Give Love*
   ✯ *Togetherness*   ✯ *The Sounds of Love*   ✯ *Loving Relationships*

652

Plant and care for a garden together. Crawling around in the dirt together has a funny way of bringing a couple closer.

653

Cook a meal *together*.

654

Listen to Garrison Keillor's *A Prairie Home Companion*, on your local public radio station, Saturday evenings from 6 to 8 p.m. If you're a fan of the Lake Wobegon stories, you'll want to tune-in. If you haven't yet discovered America's favorite humorist, you're in for a treat! Sitting quietly together and listening to the radio—instead of watching the boob tube—is a *great* change of pace.

655

Go into a bookstore together. Buy each other two books:

☞ One that you know your partner will like . . .
☞ And one that you want your partner to read.

656

☞ Take lessons together.

✳ Sailing	✳ Golfing	✳ Yoga
✳ Wind surfing	✳ Guitar	✳ Cooking
✳ Snow boarding	✳ Dancing	✳ Wine tasting

☞ Resources: Adult education organizations. Dance studios. Music studios. Cooking schools. Skydiving schools! Golf courses. Tennis clubs. City Hall. Recreation and Parks Departments.

At Home

657

Your home should be a romantic hideaway. You should be ready at a moment's notice to transform your house or apartment into a love nest through the creative use of candles, music, flowers, wine and/or good food.

658

Your home should never be without flowers. They add an elegant touch to your living room or den; they brighten up your kitchen; and they serve as a living (and aromatic) reminder of your love for one another.

659

Make a path of lighted candles leading from the front door to your bedroom. Be waiting for your lover, and let your own flame burn bright!

660

☞ Have his favorite song—or "Your Song"—playing on the stereo when he returns home from work.
☞ Play some mellow jazz, Billie Holiday, or swing music.
☞ Play his favorite dance tune at full volume with the bass cranked up!

661

Don't wait till Saturday night to go out dancing. Dance by yourselves at home in your living room.

662

Dress up for Saturday dinner at home. Ladies, wear your most elegant evening gown or party dress. Men, wear your best suit—or tuxedo if you own one. [You *could* rent one for the occasion, you know.]

663

Wash her hair for her. She'll love it. Guaranteed.

664

Carry her over the threshold of your house or apartment. (Not for newlyweds only!)

At Work

665

You do, of course, have a photo of your wife on your desk, *don't you?!*

✳ If you don't, get a nice 8-by-10 photo made, frame it, giftwrap it, and give it to yourself. Open it over breakfast with your wife, then take your gift to work with you. You'll leave her with a great memory.

✳ P.S. Place the photo *front-and-center* on your desk, not off to the side. Her smiling face will help you keep your priorities straight when you start to get stressed-out over some seemingly-important work problem.

666

Utilize your partner's secretary and staff as your allies. They can be *invaluable* in helping you spring surprises on him or her. They'll know his schedule; where she's having lunch; and whether he/she has had an especially rough day. All are crucial bits of information you should know.

667

Instruct your secretary that all calls from your wife are to be put through— regardless of what you're doing, or who you're meeting with. (*Prove* to your wife that she's the top priority in your life.)

668

Copy your face (or other body parts) on the Xerox machine. Mail it to him with a funny or suggestive note.

669

Pack a pillow and a blanket in a picnic basket and surprise your partner by appearing in the office at noon. Tell the secretary to hold all calls. Lock the office door. Turn off the intercom. Close the blinds. Make love on the desk.

670

Same as above, but pack a *real* lunch. (Not as fun, but more nutritious.)

671

Mail a greeting card to her at work.

672

Find out where he's having lunch; have flowers delivered there. (Or deliver them yourself!)

673

Ladies: Mail some of your lingerie to him—at *work*. Send him one piece of a two-piece outfit, along with an enticing love note! (Make sure you wrap it well, and include a note on the outside of the package that says "Be *alone* when you open this envelope." You want to surprise him, not embarrass him!)

674

Mail him a Rolodex card with your name and number on it. Write on it: "Call when lonely."

675

Create a "Gift & Card Drawer" in your desk at work. At all times your inventory should include: At least 10 greeting cards, lots of Love Stamps, two items of lingerie, a bunch of "Trinket Gifts," a couple of *real* gifts, plus wrapping paper and bows.

676

Make sure you find a way to do something romantic *during a time when you're the most busy at work!* (It's *easy* to be romantic when you've got all the time in the world.) A little pre-planning will allow you to be romantic and businesslike at the same time.

Around Town

677

Celebrate your own "Tourist Day." Call your local Convention and Tourist Bureau, get a pile of brochures and pamphlets, and plan to "play tourist." What sites haven't you seen? What museums have you forgotten about? What attractions were you unaware of? What cultural events have you missed?

678

Subscribe to your local city magazine—it's a *wealth* of information for romantics! They always review the best restaurants, and report on new stores and unique services. The ads are great resources, too. Don't forget to check-out the Classified Ad section.

679

Around your town are all the stores you'll need to inspire and satisfy your romantic urges. Try browsing in each of these types of shops with nothing specifically in mind . . . and see what romantic possibilities jump out at you:

- 🐛 Bookstores
- 🐛 Used bookstores
- 🐛 Card shops
- 🐛 Stationery stores
- 🐛 Toy stores
- 🐛 Lingerie shops
- 🐛 Paper stores
- 🐛 School supply stores
- 🐛 Nostalgia shops
- 🐛 Video stores
- 🐛 Music stores
- 🐛 Second-hand stores
- 🐛 Dress boutiques
- 🐛 Hotel gift shops
- 🐛 Sporting goods shops

680

Go for a "mystery drive" in the country. Keep to the back roads and ignore the map. Agree to have lunch at the first charming inn or classic diner you pass.

♥ If you stumble onto a quaint bed-and-breakfast, stay the night! (You do, of course, have "His" and "Hers" overnight bags stored in the trunk, *don't you?!*)

♥ If you keep your camping equipment in the trunk, you'll be ready for all kinds of opportunities.

681

Go for a horse-drawn carriage ride through the city—or the country.

682

Check-out the adult education programs in your area. Most programs include many one-session seminars and workshops that are fun and entertaining as well as educational.

☞ Attend a class *together:* Dancing, massage, yoga, exercise, cooking . . .

☞ . . . Or sign him up for a class you know he'll enjoy.

Creating a loving relationship
is the most difficult, time-consuming
and complicated challenge
you will face in your entire life.

~ GJPG

Dining Out

683

Did you know that there are *two* kinds of romantic restaurants?

1. The elegant/active/often-with-great-views restaurant
2. The small/dark/cozy-with-tiny-tables restaurant

Which kind of restaurant does she prefer? Don't take her to *one* when she's crazy about the *other*.

684

☞ Arrange to have a small gift delivered to your table just before the main course is served.

☞ Arrange to have a dozen red roses delivered to your table.

☞ Hire a musician to serenade your lover at your table.

685

Get to know the owner, manager or maître d' at your favorite restaurant. Become a "regular" and you'll get the best tables, best service and best wines, plus inside tips on what's *really* best on the menu tonight.

686

Get a menu from his favorite restaurant. Turn it into a "Certificate Good for One Romantic Dinner." Mail it to him at work.

687

Sunday brunch! Check the Sunday newspaper for ads. Ask your friends for their favorite spots.

688

"The Great Search for the Most Romantic Restaurant in Town." Create a list of candidates garnered from restaurant reviews in the newspaper, from ads, and tips from your friends. Visit a different restaurant every one or two weeks. Rate them according to your own personal standards.

689

A checklist of different *types* of restaurants to experience together:

- Cajun
- Cantonese
- Chinese
- French
- German
- Greek
- Hawaiian
- Vegetarian
- Irish
- Italian
- Japanese
- Mexican
- Polish
- Polynesian
- Seafood
- Steak
- Thai
- Vietnamese

690

Have lunch or dinner in an unusual place. Many museums have nice cafes. Or how about dinner at the airport? Outdoor cafes? Old-fashioned diners?

691

Get up extra-early on a weekday and go out for breakfast with your lover. It's a great way to start the day in a totally different way.

692

Find an all-night diner. They usually have the best breakfasts available anywhere, served 24-hours-a-day.

693

For a dinner that combines mystery, comedy, intrigue and music—try The Mystery Cafe! The best of the "murder mystery dinner theatres," The Mystery Cafe serves up great entertainment along with a fabulous four-course dinner. Audience participation is a *must!* The Mystery Cafe is now serving "murder" in these cities:

* Boston, Massachusetts
* Burlington, Vermont
* Nashua, New Hampshire
* North Conway, New Hampshire
* Canal Fulton, Ohio
* Columbus, Ohio
* Seattle, Washington

* Philadelphia, Pennsylvania
* Pittsburgh, Pennsylvania
* Richmond, Virginia
* Indianapolis, Indiana
* Minneapolis, Minnesota
* Newport Beach, California
* San Jose, California

If your partner is a Sherlock Holmes or Agatha Christie fan, you'll thrill him "to death" as the two of you join the other mystery-loving patrons in solving a great murder mystery.

Romantic gestures have no ulterior motive. Their only purpose is to express love.

~ GJPG

Off the Wall

694

Fake a power outage at home. (Loosen the fuses or throw the breaker switches.) Get out the candles. Then try to think of *something* to do . . .

695

Test drive a Porsche together.

696

Hide a (very) small gift somewhere on your body. Then say to your lover, "I've got a gift for you, and it's hidden on me somewhere! Find it and it's yours!" Use your imagination—and be sure to leave enough time to participate in any "extracurricular activities" that may result from the search!

697

Slow-dance at a restaurant—*when there's no music playing.* (When one man from the Romance Class did this with his girlfriend, he reported that they were applauded by the other patrons, and given a complimentary bottle of champagne by the management!)

698

Write wacky notes, memos and things, based on your profession:

* ✯ Teacher: Write a report card.
* ✯ Lawyer: Write out a summons.
* ✯ Policeman: Write a ticket.
* ✯ Executive: Write a business plan.
* ✯ Doctor: Write a prescription.
* ✯ Secretary: Write a memo.
* ✯ Salesman: Place an order.
* ✯ Truck driver: Make a packing slip.
* ✯ Anyone: Write a resumé.
* ✯ *Your* profession: Be creative!

699

* ❦ Tie a piece of string to the inside doorknob of your front door. String it throughout the house, tracing a path that leads to the bathtub, which you've prepared especially for him.
* ❦ Variation on a theme: Tie one end of the string to a body part of your choice; wait patiently in the bedroom.

700

On a budget? Create a "Disney World Vacation-At-Home"! Gather as much Mickey Mouse paraphernalia as possible: Hats and ears, stuffed animals, wind-up toys, balloons, puppets and posters. Rent some Disney movies. (*Fantasia* is available on video, you know!) [C'mon! Have some fun . . . Be a kid again!]

701

Write her a check for a million kisses.

702

Snuggle up to a roaring fire in the fireplace—in the middle of August.

703

Cool things you could rent from a "Rent-All" or "Rental World" store:

- ❦ An automatic bubble machine (like Lawrence Welk!)
- ❦ A popcorn popper (like in a movie theatre!)
- ❦ A "fogger," that makes special-effects fog
- ❦ A Victorian carriage and horse
- ❦ A pinball machine
- ❦ A jukebox

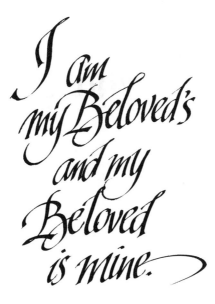

I am my Beloved's and my Beloved is mine.

Song of songs 6:3

Oldies But Goodies

704

It's getting harder and harder to find classic 45 RPM records, and it's almost impossible to locate old 78s! (As a matter of fact, since this book was first published, two companies originally listed here have disappeared.) The following firm values the classics as much as you do:

➤ House of Oldies, 35 Carmine Street, New York City, New York 11014; 212-243-0500

705

Romantic Oldies from the 1920s:

- *I'll Be with You in Apple Blossom Time*
- *Somebody Loves Me*
- *Shuffle Along*
- *Georgia*
- *Mexicali Rose*
- *Lady Be Good*
- *Rose Marie*
- *Sleepy Time Gal*
- *Why Do I Love You?*
- *I Can't Give You Anything But Love*
- *More Than You Know*
- *You Do Something to Me*
- *You're the Cream in My Coffee*

**Parents who martyr their relationship
for the sake of their children
are not doing them any
favors.**

~ GJPG

706

Romantic Oldies from the 1930s:

♥ *Body and Soul*
♥ *Little White Lies*
♥ *Dancing in the Dark*
♥ *April In Paris*
♥ *It's Only a Paper Moon*
♥ *Everything I Have Is Yours*
♥ *I Only Have Eyes for You*
♥ *Begin the Beguine*

♥ *These Foolish Things Remind Me of You*
♥ *I've Got You Under My Skin*
♥ *My Funny Valentine*
♥ *Where or When*
♥ *September Song*
♥ *I'll Never Smile Again*

707

Romantic Oldies from the 1940s:

❤ *All or Nothing at All*
❤ *The Anniversary Waltz*
❤ *My Foolish Heart*
➤ *As Time Goes By*
❤ *People Will Say We're In Love*
❤ *Dream*
❤ *Laura*

➤ *To Each His Own*
❤ *Tenderly*
❤ *Mam'selle*
❤ *Baby, It's Cold Outside*
❤ *Mona Lisa*
❤ *Don't Get Around Much Anymore*

708

Romantic Oldies from the 1950s:

✳ *There's No Tomorrow*
✳ *I Get Ideas*
✳ *Let Me Go, Lover*
✳ *Chances Are*
✳ *Somewhere Along the Way*
✳ *Stranger In Paradise*
✳ *Misty*

☆ *Don't Let the Stars Get in Your Eyes*
✳ *Moments to Remember*
✳ *Friendly Persuasion*
✳ *Three Coins in the Fountain*
✳ *The Twelfth of Never*
✳ *Tears On My Pillow*

709

Romantic Oldies from the 1960s:

➤ *If Ever I Would Leave You*
➤ *Let It Be Me*
✳ *Sunny*
➤ *What Kind of Fool Am I?*
➤ *Call Me Irresponsible*
➤ *The Days of Wine and Roses*
➤ *Unchained Melody*
➤ *She Loves You*
➤ *Red Roses For a Blue Lady*
➤ *I Fall to Pieces*
➤ *You're My Soul and Inspiration*
✳ *Good Morning Starshine*
➤ *Light My Fire*
➤ *I Never Loved a Man*

710

Romantic Oldies from the 1970s:

✳ *(They Long to Be) Close to You*
♥ *How Can You Mend a Broken Heart?*
✳ *She's a Lady*
✳ *The First Time Ever I Saw Your Face*
✳ *Behind Closed Doors*
✳ *Handy Man*
✳ *I Will Always Love You*
✳ *Still Crazy After All These Years*
✳ *Don't Go Breaking My Heart*
✳ *Nobody Does It Better*
✉ *Please, Mister Postman*
✳ *Miss You*
✳ *Always and Forever*
✳ *The Rose*

711

Get this book, it's a riot: *Happy Birthday! (You Poor Old Wreck)*, edited by Helen Exley. It's a collection of birthday messages written by young children. Some representative selections:

❝ *I like the idea of growing old, well, not too old, about nineteen or so.* ❞

❝ *Getting old is getting white hairs from worrying about your wrinkles.* ❞

❝ *Middle age is when you start watching boring things like the News.* ❞

712

Hold your own "Oldies But Goodies" nights at home. Here are some different "Themes" that Romance Class participants have tried with great success:

❖ **The 1920s:** Complete with flapper outfits and jazz.

❖ **WW II:** Complete with military uniforms, USO posters and patriotic music.

❖ **The 1960s:** Love beads, Woodstock, old jeans and tie-dyed T-shirts!

❖ **The Victorian Era:** With rented costumes, minuets and carriage rides!

713

Rent some *classic* romantic movies!

☞ *Casablanca*
☞ *Gone With The Wind*
☞ *The Philadelphia Story*
☞ *Singin' in the Rain*
☞ *Lawrence of Arabia*

☞ *West Side Story*
☞ *Romeo and Juliet*
☞ *A Streetcar Named Desire*
☞ *Doctor Zhivago*

*Your shared experiences and joint memories
weave a tapestry that combines
your two lives into one.*

~ GJPG

Games People Play

714

I've discovered that a surprising number of couples in the Romance Class play various "Car Games." Here are some of them:

✵ Kissing at every stop light.
✵ Kissing whenever you spot a red Corvette.
✵ Making love at highway rest areas.
✵ And variations of *"How Far Will You Go?"*

715

"All-Day Foreplay." Plan in the morning to make love tonight. Call each other all day long with "reminders," ideas and suggestive suggestions. By the time evening rolls around . . . !

716

"The Affair Game" or "The First Date Game." (Recommended especially for those married 10+ years.) Imagine that you're not yet married to your partner, but that you're about to have an affair (or go on your first date) with him or her. How would you act? How would you dress? How would you treat her? Where would you go? What would you do? Would you buy new clothes, lose five pounds?

717

"Romance Roulette." Randomly choose a number between 1 and 1001, then find that number in this book. The "chooser" must implement the idea during the next week. (You may want to exclude the chapter called "Spare No Expense," unless you're filthy rich!)

718

Several innovative couples play a game that goes by many different names, but generally follows the same rules. Some of the games include:

- ☞ "Who's Got It Now?"
- ☞ "Where's The Bunny?"
- ☞ "Hide-And-Go-Seek."

The rules are: Pick a small inanimate object (like a little stuffed animal, a wind-up toy, seashell, piece of plastic fruit, etc.); take turns giving it to each other in creative, funny ways. Some couples keep the object in constant rotation; others will wait *months* before giving it back, and go to *incredible* lengths to surprise their partner.

World Class players have reportedly:

- ✓ Sent objects via Federal Express.
- ✓ Had airline stewardesses deliver them while in flight.
- ✓ Had the object sealed inside Coke cans.
- ✓ Had the object appear in corporate board rooms.
- ✓ Had them delivered by a parachutist.
- ✓ Had the object frozen in an ice cube.
- ✓ Placed the object in store display windows.

719

"An Enchanting Evening." (This one's a *real* board game!) Cool, fun, and revealing! Check your local toy store, game shop, or call 800-776-7662, or write to Games Partnership Ltd., 116 New Montgomery, Suite 500, San Francisco, California 94105.

720

- ✳ **Strip poker.**
- ✳ **Strip *chess*** —for the more intellectual among you.

No-Cost Gestures

721

Even-Day/Odd-Day Romance: On *even* days it's *your* turn to be romantic, and on *odd* days it's your *partner's* turn!

722

Pick wildflowers—from a field or the side of the road.

723

Bring hotel items home: Little fancy soaps, shampoo and stuff. (I know it sounds silly, but it's really appreciated!)

724

Go wild in the kitchen! (And after you do that, cook her favorite meal for her!)

725

☞ Tape some funny newspaper headlines to his computer screen, the TV screen, her steering wheel, the telephone, the refrigerator.
☞ Stick 'em in books, magazines, drawers, shoes.
☞ Make a collage out of 'em.

726

When's the last time you sat on his lap and "made-out"??

727

What do you think would happen if every couple in America set aside every Wednesday evening to celebrate their love in some quiet, private way?

728

When's the last time you took a moonlit stroll?

729

✳ How about staging a personal Lingerie Fashion Show for him?
✳ Or how about creating a Lingerie Fashion Show *videotape* for him?!

730

Attend wine tastings at liquor stores!

731

Go through revolving doors together.

732

Unplug the TV. Put a note on the screen saying "Turn me on instead."

733

Take a favorite 45 RPM record, and paste a new label over the original one: Re-title the song, using her name or some personal reference; or simply rename it "Our Song."

Potpourri

734

Picnics! [I checked, and nowhere is it written that you can't have picnics indoors, in the nude, in front of a fireplace, in your office, in bed, on the roof of your apartment building, or at midnight.]

735

"Better Living Through Technology," Lesson #1: The VCR.

- Step 1: Figure out how to record programs on your VCR (or have the nearest youngster show you how).
- Step 2: Tape his favorite TV show.
- Step 3: Make love during that timeslot. (Hint: Choose his favorite *hour-long* show, not his favorite *half-hour* sit-com.)

736

Bake a giant chocolate chip cookie for him. [I'm talking two feet in diameter here.] If your oven's not big enough, find the most offbeat bakery in town— they'll have them.

737

Two hours of peace and quiet: *Possibly the best gift you could ever give someone!*

- ➤ Get her the book *The Quiet Answer*, by Hugh Prather, and any of Yanni's albums.
- ➤ Arrange a surprise afternoon off work for him.

738

Are you tired of running to the video store for your fix of romantic movies? Why not simply subscribe to *Love Stories-encore 2*, the premium cable TV channel that plays romantic movies 24 hours a day, 7 days a week?! Classic films as well as current flicks are featured, along with interviews with the leading authorities on love and relationships. Romance, education and convenience—what more could you ask for? Ask for *Love Stories-encore 2* (from Encore's Thematic Multiplex) by calling your local cable operator or Digital Broadcast Satellite distributor.

739

✗ Buy a copy of Louise Hay's wonderful book *You Can Heal Your Life.*
✗ Along with your partner, do several of her suggested exercises.
✗ Read her excellent chapter on "Relationships."

740

Keep candles in the car. Eat dinner by candlelight the next time you go to McDonald's or Burger King.

741

Create your own "Signature Drink"—or try one of the suggestions below. I like to start with B&B Liqueur, and experiment with fruit, spices, juices, ice cream and other liquors. Romantic? You bet!

South of France
1-1/2 oz. rum
1 oz. B&B
4 oz. pineapple juice
1-1/2 oz. Coco Lopez
Serve in a large goblet. Garnish with pineapple and a cherry.

B&B Bastille
3 oz. B&B
3 oz. lime juice
2-3 tsp. sugar

Blend in a blender. Serve with straws and a lime wheel garnish in a goblet.

What's In a Name?

742

Here are just a few women's names that are titles of popular songs:

- ❦ *Angie*, Rolling Stones
- ❦ *Anna*, The Beatles
- ❦ *Annie*, from the Musical "Annie"
- ❦ *Annie*, John Denver
- ❦ *Billie Jean*, Michael Jackson
- ❦ *Cracklin' Rosie*, Neil Diamond
- ❦ *Dear Prudence*, The Beatles
- ❦ *Dreamboat Annie*, Heart
- ❦ *Katy Lied*, Steely Dan
- ❦ *Felicia*, Herb Alpert
- ❦ *Jean*, Oliver
- ❦ *Joanna*, Kool and the Gang
- ❦ *Suite: Judy Blue Eyes*, Crosby, Stills, Nash & Young
- ❦ *Julia*, The Beatles
- ❦ *Lucy in the Sky with Diamonds*, The Beatles
- ❦ *Maria*, West Side Story
- ❦ *Marie*, Frank Sinatra & The Tommy Dorsey Orchestra
- ❦ *Martha My Dear*, The Beatles
- ❦ *Michelle*, The Beatles
- ❦ *Once in Love with Amy*, Ray Bolger
- ❦ *Peg*, Steely Dan
- ❦ *Sexy Sadie*, The Beatles
- ❦ *Sherry*, Journey/Steve Perry
- ❦ *Sweet Caroline*, Neil Diamond
- ♥ *Tracy*, The Archies

743

Do you know the *significance* of your lover's name? Here are a few samples taken from a "baby name" book:

☞ **Ada** is "joyous."

☞ **Amy** is "beloved," from the Latin.

☞ **Barbara** means "mysterious stranger."

☞ **Cathleen's** and **Kathy's** are "pure."

☞ **Diane** derives from the Latin Diana, meaning "Goddess of the Moon."

☞ **Gary** is a "mighty spear."

☞ **Gregory** is "vigilant."

☞ **Jean**, **Janet** and **Joanna** are all variations of **John** . . .

☞ **John** is "God's gracious gift."

☞ **Judy** is "admired and praised."

☞ **Kevin** is "kind and gentle."

☞ **Laurie's** and **Laurel's** are, of course, Latin for "the laurel."

☞ **Linda** is Spanish, meaning "beautiful."

☞ **Mary's** and **Maureen's** are either a "wished-for child," or "rebellious."

☞ **Monica** is an "advisor."

♥ **Tracey** is a modern version of **Teresa**, meaning "reaper."

☞ **Warren** is a "defender."

☞ **Wendy** was invented by J.M. Barrie for the heroine of Peter Pan!

744

If her name is April, May or June, declare the corresponding month "her" month, and do something special for her every day. (Every woman is "one-in-a-million," but few are "one-in-twelve"!)

745

Name your boat after her.

Guidelines

746

Timing. Timing is *everything*.

➤ Belated birthday cards ought to be outlawed.
➤ Chocolate is romantic—*but not if she's on a diet.*
➤ Stick to *small* romantic gestures when he's totally preoccupied with a big work project. (Save the biggies until he can appreciate them.)
➤ Pulling surprises requires a superb sense of timing.

747

Dot your *i*'s and cross your *t*'s. In other words, pay attention to details!

✳ Don't buy just *any* flowers—get her favorites.
✳ Make a point of *always* wrapping his gifts in his favorite color.
✳ Don't buy her *gold* jewelry when she prefers *silver*.

748

"Walk a mile in his shoes," then re-think your romantic gestures.

✦ After an especially tough week, he'd probably prefer a massage to going out to a movie.
✦ Don't bring her flowers when what she *really* needs is two hours of peace and quiet. (Two hours of peace and quiet just may be the best gift you ever give her!)

749

Remember that relationships are not self-regulating! They're delicate creations that require attention, adjustment and regular oiling.

750

Romantics are not martyrs! They don't put their partners first by ignoring their own needs and wants. Rather, they put their *relationship* first, and do things that enhance the couple as a whole. Self-sacrifice always backfires because it builds resentment in the giver and creates guilt in the receiver. Romantic gestures performed out of love provide benefits to both the giver and the receiver.

Resources

751

Catalogs are great resources. Not only for specific gifts, but also for ideas and concepts you can implement on your own. For starters, you could investigate some catalogs of catalogs!

- *America's Most Wanted Catalogs,* 951 Broken Sound Parkway NW, Building 190, Post Office Box 5057, Boca Raton, Florida 33431.
- *Shop At Home Catalogs,* 2080 South Holly Street, Post Office Box 221050, Denver, Colorado 80222.

752

Bridal magazines are great resources for finding romantic vacation destinations. (If you think that honeymoons are just for newlyweds, you're missing some great romantic opportunities!) Pick-up a copy of *Bride's, Modern Bride, Bridal Review, Bridal Trends, Bride & Groom, Brides Today* or *Bridal Guide.*

753

Some books on love, relationships, men and women, and stuff like that . . .

- 📖 *Love is Letting Go of Fear*, by Gerald Jampolsky
- 📖 *Living, Loving & Learning*, by Leo Buscaglia
- 📖 *Notes on Love and Courage*, by Hugh Prather
- 📖 *The Oxford Book of Marriage*, edited by Helge Rubinstein
- 📖 *Love*, by Leo Buscaglia
- 📖 *The Psychology of Romantic Love*, by Nathan Branden
- 📖 *You Just Don't Understand*, by Deborah Tannen, Ph.D.
- 📖 *Loving Each Other*, by Leo Buscaglia
- 📖 *Rediscovering Love*, by Willard Gaylin
- 📖 *The Tao of Relationships*, by Ray Grigg
- 📖 *Love and Will*, by Rollo May
- 📖 *Iron John*, by Robert Bly

754

Some fun and funny books about relationships, love, etc., etc., etc.

- ♠ *Dave Barry's Guide to Marriage and/or Sex*
- ♠ *Sex: If I Didn't Laugh I'd Cry*, by Jess Lair
- ♠ *The Dieter's Guide to Weight Loss During Sex*, by Richard Smith
- ♠ *The Art of Kissing*, by William Cane
- ♠ *The Hug Therapy Book*, by Kathleen Keating
- ♠ *Why Did I Marry You, Anyway?* by Arlene Modica Matthews
- ♠ *Is Sex Necessary?* by James Thurber & E.B. White

755

http://www.godek.com

756

If you're looking for info on an anniversary year, birthday year, or any other significant year in your lover's life, the following two books are invaluable!

☞ *American Chronicle*, by Lois and Alan Gordon
☞ *The Timetables of History*, by Bernard Grun

They both report history in bite-sized bits, organized one year at a time, in easy-to-scan sections such as: In the News, TV, Radio, Music, Culture, Daily Life, Sports, Science and Technology, Literature, Theatre, Fashion, Arts and Politics.

757

Resources around town. Call 'em! Ask 'em questions! Send for their catalogs and brochures!.

* Adult education programs
* Convention & Tourist Bureaus
* Dance studios
* Music studios
* Cooking schools
* Skydiving schools!

* Golf courses
* Tennis clubs
* City Hall
* Town Recreation Department
* The Parks Department

758

If you're ever desperate for tickets, call Tickets On Request. Whether it's sporting events, concerts or Broadway shows, they've got "Choice seats on short notice." These tickets ain't cheap, but they *are* the best tickets in town. The friendly folks at Tickets On Request really understand the importance of fast service—and how a couple of fabulous last-minute tickets to a sold-out show can create a memorable romantic experience! Call them at 212-967-5600, or write to them at 15 East Putnam Avenue, Suite 269, Greenwich, Connecticut 06830.

1-800-ROM-ANCE

759

800-762-6677 . . . will get you Balloon Dispatch USA. This one number gives you access to a great company that serves your balloon-o-gram needs anywhere in the country. Basic "balloon bouquets" start at $35 (plus delivery), and fancier deliveries can run into the hundred-dollar range. For example, you can get "singing balloon-o-grams," or a mini gondola-like balloon with a hanging basket filled with champagne, flowers or gifts. One-day notice is adequate.

760

800-ALL-BOOK . . . will get you—books!! All books, all titles, all publishers, all hours of the day or night. (In Connecticut, 203-966-5470.)

761

800-9999-VIP . . . will get you exotic vacations and worldwide travel and romantic adventures! "The name says it all" at V I P Travel Service, where every client is treated like a V.I.P. Call them for vacation suggestions, romantic get-aways, and adventures big and small.

❦❦❦❦❦❦❦❦❦❦

Give your lover 15 minutes of undivided attention every day.

~ GJPG

❦❦❦❦❦❦❦❦❦❦

762

800-543-1949... will get you started on a romantic trip on a Mississippi riverboat. The Delta Queen Steamboat Company in New Orleans operates the Mississippi Queen and the Delta Queen.

763

800-AH-KAUAI . . . will get you information on the breathtakingly romantic Hawaiian island of Kauai.

764

Go cruisin' . . .

❦ *Carnival Cruises*	*800-327-7276*
❦ *Commodore Cruise Line*	*800-832-1122*
❦ *Cunard Line*	*800-221-4770*
❦ *Norwegian Cruise Line*	*800-327-7030*
❦ *Premier Cruise Line*	*800-327-7113*
❦ *Princess Cruises*	*800-LOVEBOAT*
❦ *Royal Viking Cruises*	*800-426-0821*
❦ *Windjammer Barefoot Cruises*	*800-327-2601*
❦ *Windstar Sail Cruises*	*800-258-7245*

765

✧ As they say, "Virginia Is For Lovers." To find out if it's true, call 800-527-6517.

✧ And if you ♥ NY, call 800-225-5697.

766

800-423-9494 . . . will get you the Playboy catalog. It's full of cool gift ideas.

- ❦ You can get a classic issue of Playboy Magazine from a specific month and year to commemorate a significant event in your/his/her life. (For those of you who really *do* "read the articles," the catalog notes each issue's interview or special feature.) Copies are available back through February of 1961.
- ❦ You can get Vargas posters and a variety of Playboy insignia items.
- ❦ You can also get a variety of videos, too. The massage videos are surprisingly good. Informative and tasteful. (*Explicit* . . . but tasteful.)
- ❦ And, of course, you can get lingerie.

767

800-284-JAVA. . . will get you coffee delivered to your doorstep! Just like a subscription to your favorite magazine, you can get a subscription to exotic coffees from around the world. The Coffee Connection's mail order subscription service will deliver your selections every one, two, three or four weeks—to suit your coffee-drinking habits. In addition to coffee from the Americas, you can get offerings from Africa, Arabia, Indonesia and the Pacific.

768

800-BE-THERE. . . will get you one of the leading gift delivery services. The firm, 800 Spirits, specializes in delivering champagne, fine wines, liquors, cordials and gourmet foods. As they say, if you can't be there in person, be there in spirit! Call for their $3, 48-page catalog.

769

✳ For sci-fi fans: *The Science Fiction Video Catalog:* 800-959-0061
✳ For pet lovers: *Mail Order Pet Shop Catalog:* 800-326-6677
✳ For picky snackers: *The Ace Specialty Foods Catalog:* 800-635-2186
✳ For personalized gifts: *Initials Catalog:* 800-225-8390
✳ For hot air balloon fans! *In The Air Catalog:* 800-583-8038

770

800-352-3800 . . . will get you information on how to cross the Atlantic in true luxury aboard the amazing Queen Elizabeth 2. The QE2 isn't fast, but who wants to rush one of the most romantic modes of transportation ever devised by man?

771

800-423-4038 . . . connects you with The Clambake Company, on Cape Cod. This one is *great*. They'll send you an *entire lobster feast* including the pots and utensils—air expressed overnight to any location! The traditional New England seafood dinner-for-two includes: two 1-1/4 pound lobsters; 1-1/2 pounds of steamers; a pound of mussels; two ears of fresh corn; four to six red bliss potatoes; two chunks of onion; and two links of sweet Italian sausage. Price—including shipping and lobster bibs—is $136. Ask for their Clambakes-To-Go specials. (In Massachusetts, call 508-255-3289.)

Relationships aren't 50/50—they're 100/100.

- GJPG

Mementos

772

Have you saved any old love letters you've sent to each other? Dust them off and re-read them. Maybe read them aloud to each other. Revive the memories; re-experience your love as it was when it was new.

773

❦ Vow to start saving mementos of your life together.
❦ Create a "Mementos File" or "Memories Box."

774

Stuff to save:

☞ Movie stubs, theatre programs, restaurant receipts
☞ Sand and seashells from your beach vacations
☞ Labels from wine bottles and corks from champagne bottles
☞ Restaurant menus and placemats

775

✴ Page through your photo albums together on a rainy afternoon.
✴ Turn your favorite pictures into a "Video Photo Album."
  (See #923.)

The Golden Rules of Romance

776

The receiver defines what's romantic.

✳ If you give her flowers, and she hates flowers, it ain't romantic.
✳ If you've spent all day cooking a gourmet meal, and he'd rather call Domino's for a pizza . . . guess what?
✳ If you've spent a fortune on an outfit for her, and she says it isn't her style, you have no right to be resentful.

777

Time and effort expended are usually more appreciated than money spent.

778

Romantics give their relationship the top priority in their lives.

Everything else flows *from* the relationship, *through* the relationship, and *because of* the primary love relationship, if your life is operating in a successfully dynamic manner. This does not mean that one becomes a martyr on behalf of the other. Martyrs hurt themselves, and thus harm the relationship. Healthy relationships always support and nurture the individual.

779

Romantic gestures have no ulterior motive.

Their only purpose is to express love; to show that she's important and special to you; to let him know that you think about him often.

780

Planning doesn't destroy spontaneity—it creates opportunity.

781

☆ *The un-asked-for gift is most appreciated.*
☆ *The surprise gift is most cherished.*

782

The Romantic Law of Inverse Proportions:

✦ *The more you need romance in your life, the less likely you are to do it; the less you need it, the more likely you are to do it.*

The Mathematics of Romance

783

Relationships aren't 50/50. They're 100/100.

You each must take 100% responsibility for the relationship. Nobody can give 100% of themselves 100% of the time—it's impossible. But you *can* aim for it, and when you (inevitably) fall short, it'll still be okay. Even if you each fall short by as much as 50%, you'll still be in fine shape; it'll still add up to something close to 100%. The problem is when you're both trying to limit your giving to "your fair share"—usually defined as 50%. If you do that, you'll *definitely* fall short of 100%.

❧ Write little reminders to help both of you adjust your thinking. Write "100/100" on Post-It Notes, and post them all over the place for a few weeks.

784

5 minutes devoted to romance = 1 day of harmony

Think of all the times that your failure to do some little thing—like calling to tell her you'll be home late from work, or mailing her birthday card on time—has caused a full day of unhappiness. Consistent attention to your lover will keep your relationship balanced and happy. It doesn't take much! Little gestures go a long way.

785

Figure out how many days you've been together! (Don't forget to add in Leap Years.) In 10 years you'll have spent 3,652 days together! Reflect on the highlights of your time together. How have you changed? What have you accomplished together?

☞ Write a short piece, sharing your feelings about your time together.
☞ Create a timeline, noting highlights of your relationship.
☞ Try to recapture the passion and newness of your early relationship, and combine it with the depth and intimacy you've acquired over the years.

786

✻ Celebrate your *1,000th* day together.
   (That's about 2 years and 9 months.)

✻ Celebrate your *10,000th* day together.
   (That's about 27 years, 4 months and 25 days—give or take a few days, depending on when the Leap Years fall.)

Passive people never live passionate lives.

~ GJPG

Gift Ideas

787

Get your honey two small gifts and one big one . . . two red gifts and three green ones . . . one expensive gift and four inexpensive ones.

788

You'll find hundreds of great gift items in a fabulous catalog called The Celebration Fantastic. "Celebrate life's special occasions with romance, whimsy and imagination!" Everything in this catalog is just a little bit special. Items include a personalized Limoge ring box, sachets, picture frames, sterling silver items, quill pen sets, plus vases, unique cards, goblets, personalized wine bottles, pillows, sterling bar tools, quality travel bags, a really wild hand-painted birthday shirt, and a complete gourmet picnic basket. Call for a free catalog: 800-527-6566.

789

B.Y.O.B. (Brew Your Own Beer)! Now, beer connoisseurs and do-it-your-selfers can brew their own beer at home. You can do it with a kit from The Sharper Image catalog. [But is it romantic? Well, I'm not sure. But . . .] Call them at 800-344-4444.

790

Get her something that she's always wanted to have, but always held back on . . . because it was too expensive, too impractical, too weird or too self-indulgent.

791

Music boxes! Find them in a local gift shop, or get a phenomenal catalog from The San Francisco Music Box Company. Call 800-227-2190. Their music boxes are beautiful, and they have hundreds and *hundreds* of songs to choose from!

792

Satin sheets!

793

Gifts for *her:* Anything from Crabtree and Evelyn. Take my word for it. Visit a nearby bath shop, or find a Crabtree and Evelyn boutique, or call them at 800-289-1222.

794

For a musical touch of class, how about a recording called *Amore: The Great Italian Love Arias!?* It's a collection of 23 of the world's most beautiful love songs from 15 of the world's greatest operas—La Boheme, Tosca, Madama Butterfly, Turandot, Rigoletto, Aida, Pagliacci, L'Elisir d'amore, and others, sung by international stars Kiri te Kanawa, Luciano Pavarotti, Eva Marton, Richard Tucker, and Ileana Cotrubas. It's available on CDs and cassettes.

795

Make a collage for her. The theme: Her favorite fairy tale. Clip illustrations from several different books. Intersperse photos of the two of you! Combine classic verses from the story with phrases from your own lives.

796

Creative gift wrapping:

☞ Use Sunday comics for wrapping paper.
☞ Use cartons of Ben & Jerry's Ice Cream for boxes.

797

Doesn't he deserve a trophy for being the "World's Best Lover"? Doesn't she merit a loving cup to celebrate her latest accomplishment? Trophy shops have a wealth of ideas waiting for you: Plaques, medals, ribbons, nameplates, certificates and banners. And they're all personalized, engraved, lettered or monogrammed. Check the Yellow Pages under "Trophies"!

798

Get gift items to go along with your pet names for each other:

✜ *Babe*	✜ *FuzzyFace*	✜ *Lover*	✜ *Playmate*
✜ *Big Bear*	✜ *Gumdrop*	✜ *Macho Man*	✜ *Pussycat*
✳ *Bunny*	✜ *Honey bun*	✜ *Muffin*	✜ *Sweetie*
✜ *Cookie*	✜ *Jellybean*	✳ *Peeper*	✜ *Teddybear*
✳ *Sweet Pea*	✜ *Kitten*	✜ *Piglet*	✜ *Tiger*

799

Don't forget about charm bracelets! They bring good memories alive, and they provide a built-in gift idea for any occasion.

800

How about a copy of the front page of a newspaper from the date of his birth, or from your anniversary date? Photocopies of thousands of U.S. newspapers are available from Bell & Howell Microprints.

✯ An actual newspaper-size print, 17-by-23-inches, is $38.50
✯ An 8-by-10-inch print is $27.50

Call 800-521-0600, or write to 300 North Zeeb Road, Ann Arbor, Michigan 48106.

801

Run down to your local bookstore. Buy one of those journal books. Every day or every other day, write down your thoughts about her, about your relationship, about your lives together. Some days you'll just jot a quick "I love you"—other days you may be inspired to write page after page. Do this for an entire year! Then present it to her on your anniversary or her birthday.

802

Here's a selection of "New Age" music which ranges from mellow acoustic guitar solos to melodic piano solos to amazing electric harp pieces to . . .

➢ Andreas Vollenweider: *Down to the Moon*
➢ David Lanz: *Heartsounds; Seasons; Impressions; Pianoscapes*
➢ George Winston: *Autumn; Winter Into Spring; Summer*
➢ Justo Almario: *Forever Friends*
➢ Liz Story: *Solid Colors*
➢ Paul Winter: *Sun Singer; WinterSong*
➢ William Ackerman: *Past Light; It Takes A Year; Childhood & Memory*
➢ Windham Hill Artists: *A Winter's Solstice; A Winter's Solstice II*
➢ Yanni: *Reflections of Passion; Keys to Imagination; Out of Silence*

The Gift of Time

803

Give her the gift of time:

❀ Get up with the kids on Saturday morning; let her sleep in.
❀ Do some of "her" chores: Go grocery shopping, weed the garden, wash the dishes.
❀ Run a bubble bath for her.

804

Give *him* the gift of time:

❀ Pay the bills, balance the checkbook.
❀ Do some of "his" chores: Cut the lawn, change the car oil, clean the basement.
❀ Spend time preparing his favorite hard-to-make meal.

805

The gift of time:

☞ Two hours of peace and quiet
☞ A day without the kids
☞ Sunday morning in bed together
☞ Saturday afternoon . . .
☞ A weekend get-away
☞ A little "afternoon delight"
☞ Taking time out
☞ Taking a "movie-break"

806

"Double-up" on activities. Combine various activities and you'll find more time to be together:

* Meet for lunch. (You have to eat anyway, right?!)
* Eat dinner and watch a romantic movie on video.
* Do a chore *together.* Go grocery shopping, take the car to the shop.

807

Time and effort expended are usually more appreciated than money spent. Your partner wants more of you, not more **stuff.** Once every two months give her an entire day of your time. To do with whatever she wants. Now, ask her for the same, during the alternate months. Just *imagine* the possibilities!

808

Practice "chore-shifting." Don't go grocery shopping on *Friday night!* Don't do laundry on *Saturday morning!* Those are **valuable** times—times you could be spending *together.*

* Find ways to shift chores to more efficient times.
* Do two chores at the same time.
* Do chores *together:* Doubling the personpower more than doubles the efficiency!

809

* Hire a caterer to serve dinner at home—just for the two of you.
* Bring home Chinese take-out or pizza once a week.
* Hire a housecleaning service.

810

Planning! *Planning doesn't destroy spontaneity—it creates opportunity!*

✶ Review your calendars and commitments together. Plan "dates."
✶ Plan surprises well in advance.
✶ Always have your "Gift Closet" well stocked. (See #48)

811

✳ You can *save* time by shopping via catalog.
✳ You can *reorganize* time by "chore-shifting."
✳ You can *create* time by "doubling up" on activities.
✳ You can *use time more efficiently* by buying a book on time management.
✳ You can *release* time by hiring a housecleaning service.
✳ You can *find* time by planning better.

812

Make time in the morning to make love. Get up an hour early!

Break Out of That Box!

813

Do something *totally out of character.*

✓ **Always late?**—Be on time.
✓ **Not creative?**—Think-up something original and unexpected!
✓ **Forgetful?**—Remember her birthday *every day for a month!*
✓ **Watch TV every night?**—Go out to dinner instead.

814

Don't let yourself be constrained by your employer's tightwad two-week vacation policy. If you want to take-off for a month-long trekking vacation in Nepal, *do it!* Simply take two weeks off without pay. What's the big deal?! (If you have the dream but not the dough, then plan for it! Create a savings plan that will allow you to amass the required cash. Where there's a will there's a way.)

Romance is a process—it's not an event.

~ GJPG

815

Are you stuck in a rut? Are you taking each other for granted lately? Try "re-framing." Re-frame, or re-define, how you see your partner.

❤ Start thinking of her as *your lover* once again.
❤ Start treating him like your *best friend*, which he probably was at one time.

816

Act out different fantasies of meeting for the first time:

✳ Meet in a bar after work.
✳ Meet while grocery shopping.
✳ Meet in line, waiting at the bank.
✳ Meet over lunch at work.

817

Are you stuck in a boring routine every evening? (Home from work; run some errands; grab some dinner; pay some bills; watch some TV; crawl into bed.) *Radically change your routine:*

✯ Visit someplace within an hour's drive of your home that you've never been to before.

✯ Bring dinner home from a take-out Chinese or pizza place, then head for an early movie.

✯ Meet after work at the local art museum; eat at the cafe there; spend the evening browsing with the high-brow.

✯ Meet at the mall; go window shopping; dine at your favorite fast food joint.

818

There's no better way to "break out of the box" than to get in touch with the child inside yourself. That little kid is playful, creative, curious, spontaneous, trusting and imaginative! Stop being such an *adult*, and re-capture those childlike qualities that really are so endearing to your partner.

☞ Suggested reading:

❖ *I'm OK—You're OK*, by Eric Berne
❖ *A Book of Games*, by Hugh Prather
❖ *Ain't I A Wonder . . . And Ain't You a Wonder Too!* by Jess Lair
❖ *The Tao of Pooh*, by Benjamin Hoff

819

Exhibitionism For The Shy. What an enticing book title! What a cool concept! This awesome book demonstrates how to turn sexual modesty to your erotic advantage! As author Carol Queen says, "To discover a new world of erotic experience, you don't have to shed your inhibitions—you just have to exploit them creatively." This book is a serious exploration and guide book. (No sleazy pictures. In fact, no pictures at all!) In local bookstores or call 800-289-8423.

820

If you're especially inept in the kitchen you've got a great opportunity to surprise your partner. *Cook a gourmet meal!* Send your partner out for the afternoon. Enlist the help of a friend who cooks. Prepare your lover's favorite dish. *Voilà!*

✳ Note: Lobster is very easy yet very classy.
✳ And, of course, there's always gourmet pizza!

821

Spend an "all-nighter" together: Make love, watch videos, go out to an all-night diner, go for a moonlit stroll, make love again, watch old movies on TV, blast the stereo and dance at 3:00 a.m. Then sleep all day the next day.

822

Switch "roles" with your lover for a day, a weekend or a week. You'll gain new insights into your partner's life—insights that will help you make romantic gestures that are more personal, intimate, appropriate and appreciated.

❖❖❖❖❖❖❖❖❖❖❖

You can't control a relationship.
It's not like driving a car—it's more like
flying a kite: You have some say
in where it goes, but not a lot!

~ GJPG

❖❖❖❖❖❖❖❖❖❖❖

Memorize This List!

823

You need to know *all* of your lover's favorite things. Here's a list. Fill in the blanks. Add additional items!

1. **Favorite color** _____

2. **Lucky number** _____

3. *Favorite flower* _____

4. *Favorite perfume* _____

5. **Favorite author** _____

6. **Favorite book** _____

7. **Favorite fairy tale** _____

8. **Favorite children's book** _____

9. **Favorite Bible passage** _____

10. **Favorite saying/verse/proverb** _____

11. *Favorite song* _____

12. *Favorite singer* _____

13. *Favorite musical band* _____

14. *Favorite kind of music* _____

15. *Favorite dance tune* _____

16. **Favorite magazine** _____

Memorize This List (cont.)

17. *Favorite cookie* _____

18. *Favorite ice cream* _____

19. *Favorite kind of chocolate* _____

20. *Favorite snack food* _____

21. Favorite restaurant (expensive) _____

22. Favorite restaurant (cheap) _____

23. Favorite fast food joint _____

24. *Favorite TV show (current)* _____

25. *Favorite TV show (old)* _____

26. Favorite comedian _____

27. Favorite actor/actress _____

28. Favorite movie _____

29. Favorite Broadway play _____

30. Favorite musical _____

31. Favorite show tune _____

32. *Favorite breed of dog* _____

33. *Favorite breed of cat* _____

34. Favorite comic strip & cartoon character _____

35. Favorite artist _____

36. Favorite style of artwork _____

Memorize This List (too)

---

37. Favorite hero/heroine/role model _____

38. Favorite athlete _____

39. Favorite sport (to watch) _____

40. Favorite sport (to play) _____

41. Favorite sports teams _____

42. *Favorite position* _____

43. *Favorite foreplay activity* _____

44. *Favorite season* _____

45. *Favorite time of day* _____

46. Favorite hobby _____

47. Favorite type of jewelry _____

48. Preferred style of clothing _____

49. Dream vacation spot _____

50. Favorite wine/champagne/liqueur _____

51. Favorite meal/favorite food _____

52. *Fill-in-the-blank favorites* _____

_____

_____

_____

_____

Miscellany

824-825

✷ Add to his collection of baseball cards, baseball caps, bottle caps, fine wines, comic books, *New Yorker* magazines.

✷ Add to her collection of dolls, stamps, salt and pepper shakers, matchbooks, stuffed animals.

826-827

☞ Visit a museum giftshop for a poster print by her favorite artist.

☞ Get the whole "family of products" in the fragrance of her favorite perfume (bath powder, soaps, cremes, candles, etc.)

828

For each letter of the alphabet, write-down three possible romantic gifts or concepts. Use this list for generating romantic ideas! [Inspired while eating *Alpha-Bits* for breakfast this morning.]

829

Make a giant greeting card out of a big cardboard box.

830-831

♣ Get *every recording ever made* by his favorite musical group.

♣ Buy her *every book ever written* by her favorite author.

832

Hold an at-home Video Film Festival, with every movie starring her favorite actor or actress.

833

Take into account whether she's a "Morning Person" or "Late-Night Person" when planning activities and surprises.

834

Wrap all her gifts in her favorite color.

835

Prepare a special meal to celebrate the beginning of each new season. (Why wait for the "official holidays"?)

836

Hire an artist to create a poster illustrating her favorite fairy tale or children's story—and have *her* pictured as the heroine!

837-838

➤ "Diamonds are a girl's best friend." Get her one!

➤ "Dogs are a man's best friend." Get him one!

839

Get the book *Love Signs*, by Linda Goodman. It contains astrological descriptions of every possible pairing of the 12 Signs of the Zodiac!

840-841

☞ Get her a pair of tickets to hear her favorite musician in concert.

☞ Get him Season Tickets for his favorite professional sports team.

842

Get a set of comedy videos that you know will really crack him up: Monty Python, Robin Williams, Abbott and Costello, The 3 Stooges.

843

Items to insert inside loveletter envelopes: Confettti ✳ A lock of your hair ✳ Feathers ✳ Stickers ✳ Heart shapes ✳ Your finger prints

844-846

♥ Buy three ties for him: One conservative/business tie, one fashionable/casual tie, and one truly OutRagEous tie.

♥ Buy a video camera for him. It'll help you capture the memories.

♥ Buy 100 Love Stamps.

Go Away!

847

❦ Visit all 50 states—one or two a year for as long as it takes.

❦ Camp in every National Park in the country.

❦ Then, start on the State Parks.

848

Go on a cruise. Take your lover and experience "The Love Boat" for yourself. Princess Cruises operates many luxury cruise ships, including the *Pacific Princess*—the ship on which the popular TV show was filmed. Call your travel agent or call 800-LOVE-BOAT.

849

Cross Canada by rail! You can travel 2,700 miles from Toronto to Vancouver in restored Art Deco train cars. The trains feature dome cars, which give panoramic views of the spectacular scenery. Call VIA Rail at 416-366-8411.

850

*A vacation is just a vacation—but a **romantic** vacation is a **honeymoon!*** (Regardless of whether or not you're a newlywed!) One of my most recent favorite romantic discoveries is ***Honeymoon*** magazine. It's described as "The magazine dedicated to planning the perfect romantic adventure." It's an *incredible* romantic resource! Its articles are as specific and practical as they are inspiring and romantic. My favorite section includes destination articles and resort profiles, and is printed on *perforated pages,* so you can easily rip out information for planning your upcoming romantic adventure. Is this practical, or what?! *Honeymoon* is a quarterly publication that can be found at most newsstands. Or call for a subscription: 800-513-7112.

851

Combine your interest in bicycling with your passion for wine! Tour the California wine country *by bike.* Pedal at your own pace, and stop at as many as 35 wineries. These two firms offer five-day guided bicycle tours through the Napa Valley and Sonoma County:

* Backroads Bicycle Touring, 800-245-3874
* Vermont Bicycle Touring, 802-453-4811

852

Here's an interesting twist: Instead of paying for hotels, exchange houses with another family! These firms will do the organizing for you:

* The Vacation Exchange Club: 800-638-3841
* Loan-A-Home, 2 Park Lane 6E, Mount Vernon, New York 10552

853

Before going on vacation, get piles of brochures, posters and books about your upcoming destination. Send them to him in a constant and varied stream of mail.

854

♠ Tour a vineyard.

♠ Visit a vineyard in every state that produces wine—all 42 of them!

855

✦ Go bodysurfing! The place to go is California's Balboa Peninsula—off Newport Beach—where 2-1/2 miles of beautiful beach lead to the world-famous "Wedge."

✦ Take a death-defying hike through Death Valley, California! (If you go in the winter, the temperature averages a not-so-deathly 60 degrees, even at noon!)

Movie Madness

856

Present her with a framed movie poster from her all-time-favorite movie! Vintage or current, romantic, dramatic or funny! Among the favorites are *Gone With The Wind; Casablanca; 2001: A Space Odyssey; 9 1/2 Weeks* and *Out of Africa.* Prices vary depending on availability, size, age and condition. Call Jerry Ohlinger's Movie Material Store at 212-989-0869. They have a vast ("thousands and thousands") assortment of stuff from the 1930s to the present. Visit their amazing shop at 242 West 14th Street, New York, New York 10011.

857

Hold an At-Home Video Film Festival! Rent the videos, pop the popcorn, clear the calendar, and roll!

❤ Some **romantic** favorites:

☞ A Man and a Woman
☞ An Officer and a Gentleman
☛ Casablanca
☞ Desert Hearts
☞ Enemies, A Love Story
☞ From Here to Eternity
☞ Funny Girl
☞ Ghost
☞ Gone With The Wind
☞ Love Story
☞ On Golden Pond
☞ I.Q.
☞ Splash
☞ Annie Hall

☞ Out of Africa
☞ Romeo and Juliet
☞ Somewhere In Time
☞ Splendor in the Grass
☞ The Accidental Tourist
☞ The Apartment
☞ The French Lieutenant's Woman
☞ The Way We Were
☞ To Have and Have Not
☛ West Side Story
☞ When Harry Met Sally
☞ French Kiss
☞ Tootsie
☞ Sleepless In Seattle

✘ Some **erotic** favorites:

➤ Body Heat
➤ 9 1/2 Weeks
➤ Dangerous Liaisons
➤ The Big Easy
➤ Crimes of Passion

➤ Henry and June
➤ Sea of Love
➤ Story of O
➤ The Fabulous Baker Boys
➤ The Lovers

ᖚᖚᖚᖚᖚᖚᖚᖚᖚᖚᖚ

Love doesn't teach, it shows the way.
Love doesn't lecture, it just loves!

~ GJPG

ᖚᖚᖚᖚᖚᖚᖚᖚᖚᖚᖚ

858

Your At-Home Video Film Festival *could* revolve around your partner's favorite movie stars:

☆ Movies starring his favorite actress: Kim Basinger, Marilyn Monroe, Barbra Streisand, Katharine Hepburn, Rita Hayworth, Greta Garbo, Lauren Bacall, Audrey Hepburn, Michelle Pfeiffer, Bette Davis, Helen Hayes, Demi Moore, Meryl Streep.

☆ Movies starring her favorite actor: Mickey Rourke, Robert Redford, Spencer Tracy, Clark Gable, Cary Grant, Warren Beatty, Dustin Hoffman, Mel Gibson, Sean Connery, Tom Cruise, Kurt Russell, Tony Curtis, Marlon Brando, Frank Sinatra, Patrick Swayze, Steve McQueen.

859

Or create "themes" for your At-Home Video Film Festivals. Choose your lover's favorite "type" or genre of movie:

◇ Comedy
✦ Science fiction
◇ Classics of the 1930s
◇ Films of the 1940s
◇ Movies of the 1950s
◇ Flicks of the 1960s

◇ All the Beatles' movies
◇ All the Neil Simon movies
◇ All of Woody Allen's movies
◇ The Elvis movies
✦ All the Pink Panther movies
◇ The James Bond movies

860

Don't neglect the many classic film series hosted by local colleges and universities, YMCAs, museums, and classic theatres.

861

And don't forget about drive-ins!

Starstruck!

862

If you'd like to spend a romantic summer night making wishes on falling stars, mark the second week in August on your calendar. The earth passes through the Perseides Meteor Belt around August 12th every year, which usually results in *spectacular* shows. (You may want to plan an evening of stargazing for the 12th, without telling her about the Perseides. She'll hardly believe her eyes when more than 100 stars per hour fall out of the sky!)

863

Speaking of falling stars . . . Those that make it all the way to the ground are called meteorites, and some of them are collected and sold by a unique shop called Strata. The meteorites range in size from dust-sized grains, to pebbles and chunks—with the most common types (iron) costing about 40¢ per gram, and the more rare specimens going for $400 per gram! The shop specializes in turning these space stones into unique jewelry and unusual gifts. Rings, pendants, earrings, paperweights and executive desk sets are most popular. Call owners John Barbieri and Will McGrath at 800-466-2992, or write to 326 Washington Street, Wellesley, Massachusetts 02181.

864

If the bright city lights ruin the romantic sport of stargazing in your neighborhood, plan your next vacation at the Star Hill Inn, located out West where the sky is bigger and more spectacular, in Sapello, New Mexico. The Star Hill Inn has been a well-kept secret of amateur astronomers and star-gazers for several years. At 7,200 feet above sea level, and far enough east of Santa Fe to be unaffected by the nighttime glare, the Inn caters to its clientele with an observation deck, star maps and a well-stocked astronomy library. Cabins with all the modern conveniences (except TVs!) are reasonably priced. Call your hosts Phil and Blair Mahon at 505-425-5605.

865

If your interest in the ✩ stars is more mystical, call Eric Linter, one of the best ✩ astrologers on the East Coast. While well-versed in the basics of birth charts and astrological ✩ predictions, Eric has a dual focus on "spiritually-oriented" astrology readings and on "couple ✩ dynamics." He prepares individual ✩ charts, couples' charts and special-purpose readings. Many couples ask him for advice on when to get ✩ engaged, and suggestions for specific dates and times to get ✩ married. You can reach Eric in Boston at ✩ 617-524-5275.

866

If it's the stars of *Broadway* that interest your partner, why not get him a poster from his favorite show? Today's and yesterday's Broadway hits are represented at the Triton Gallery, 323 West 45th Street, New York City, New York 10036. Call them at 212-765-2472 or 800-626-6674.

867

You may not be able to give her the moon and the stars, but you *can* name a star after her! The International Star Registry will provide you with a beautiful certificate that notes the star's coordinates and its new name, plus star maps and stargazing information. At $45 per star, it makes a great, unique gift for that person you're starry-eyed over. Call the International Star Registry at 800-282-3333, or write to 34523 Wilson Road, Ingleside, Illinois 60041.

868

If your lover would love to watch a space shuttle (or other rocket) launch, call NASA for timetables and other information:

✦ 407-867-INFO . . . will get you launch information.

✦ 407-867-2622 . . . will get you a base pass so you can watch a rocket launch from close-up!

✦ 407-867-2468 . . . will get you NASA Public Information.

✦ 407-452-2121 . . . will connect you with Space Port U.S.A., at the Kennedy Space Center.

Do It Outside

869

Watch the sunset together. Find a hill. Bring a picnic. It's better than TV!

870

In the winter, warm-up her car for her! And while you're at it, brush the snow off her windshield, too.

871

Go whitewater rafting! Adventurous folks at these firms will get you started downstream:

➣ Appalachian Wildwaters: 800-624-8060
➣ USA Raft: 800-USA-RAFT
➣ Outback Expeditions: 800-343-1640

872

Bicycle across the United States! The 4,500-mile TransAmerica Bicycle Trail follows side roads and uncrowded state routes through rural America. The trail goes from Yorktown, Virginia to Astoria, Oregon, and takes from 50 to 90 days to complete. In-between you pedal through Kentucky, Illinois, Missouri, Kansas, Colorado, Wyoming, Montana, Idaho and Oregon—enjoying the Rocky Mountains, Yellowstone Park, and the natural beauty of America along the way. For more information, call Adventure Cycling at 406-721-8719, or write to P.O. Box 8308, Missoula, Montana 59807. Bicyclists recommend May and June as the best months for embarking on this trip-of-a-lifetime!

873

(Make love in the back yard at night.)

874

Go camping! Borrow friends' equipment for starters. If you enjoy it, buy your own stuff. (Make sure you include a *double* sleeping bag on your equipment list.)

875

When's the last time you played Miniature Golf? Go match your skill and have a good time. [A modest suggestion for the ladies: If you're not a great golfer, wear a skimpy outfit. You'll distract him—and possibly cause him to miss a few shots. You'll also show him that you have attributes that are more important than eye-hand coordination!]

876

Go hiking. Go tobogganing! Go to a ballgame. Go to a State Park. Go to an outdoor public garden. Go to an outdoor band concert. Go on a picnic. Go for a ride in the country. Go for a walk. Go for it!

Do It In Public

877

✭ Do you praise her in public? Complimenting her in front of someone else will make her feel extra special.

✭ When's the last time you told someone else how lucky you feel to have this woman in your life?

878

Whisper sweet nothings in her ear while out in public.

➤ Whisper compliments; call her by her pet name.

➤ Whisper shocking comments and outright lewd suggestions! [The more formal the gathering, the more outrageous or suggestive your whispered messages should be. The juxtaposition of a stuffy event with the whispered raw passion of your feelings for her should add a little spark to the entire evening!]

879

If your lover's not shy, you might want to try *nude sunbathing*. Practitioners praise the sense of freedom, healthfulness and back-to-nature benefits of baring it all in public.

❧ *Free Beaches,* a bestselling (250,000 copies sold) guide to nude beaches located around the world, is available for $28, plus $4 for shipping. Call The Naturist Society at 414-426-5009; or write to Post Office Box 132, Oshkosh, Wisconsin 54902.

❧ Call the American Association for Nude Recreation at 800-879-6833; or write to 1703 North Main Street, Kissimmee, Florida 34744.

880

Do you remember what teenagers used to call "PDAs"—Public Displays of Affection? Are you out of the habit of showing affection for your partner in public? Hold hands. Rest your hand on his shoulder. Entwine your arm with hers. (Now that you're older and wiser, you know the difference between "affection" and "passion," right . . . ?)

881

. . . If you *don't* know the difference between "affection" and "passion," you just might want to consider *really* "doing it in public." The danger of being caught, and the varied settings will add a thrill to your lovemaking like you haven't experienced since you first took up the sport! Here are some favorite locations experienced by Romance Class participants (who wish to remain anonymous!):

✖ In the car
✖ In State Parks
✖ At highway rest stops

✖ At wedding receptions
✖ In apple orchards
✖ In elevators

882

Flirt with her at a party, as if you both were single.

* For beginners: Flirt just a little. Wink. Compliment her.
* For intermediate students: Act out a complete "pick-up" fantasy, without any of the other guests being aware of what you're doing.
* For advanced students: Continue the fantasy as you return home!
* For students wanting extra credit: Act out the complete "pick-up" fantasy at the party—and sneak off to an empty room, porch or closet, and make mad, passionate love!

883

For women only: When you're dressed up and out together, secretly hand him your panties under the table. Watch his expression. [If he's not *absolutely delighted*, he needs help. Serious help.]

884

Place an ad in the Personal Column of your local newspaper. Let your lover know why he or she is so special. Write it in "code," possibly using your private pet name for her. This is a great opportunity to exercise your creativity and express your feelings in just a few clever words.

* When the ad appears, circle it and leave it on the kitchen table when you leave for work.
* Or call him at work on the day the ad appears, and tell him there's a secret message for him on a certain page of the morning newspaper.

Do-It-Yourself

885

Learn to play the guitar just well enough to accompany yourself as you sing a favorite lovesong. Now serenade her!

886

Make a "This Is Your Life" videotape. Interview his friends and family, neighbors, high school teachers, college buddies, fraternity brothers, ex-girlfriends, colleagues and co-workers.

887

Write a song ✏ Pen a poem ✏ Write a love letter ✏ Jot a love note

888

Make a custom certificate for your lover. You can get blank certificate forms at any good stationery or paper store. It doesn't have to be artistic and perfect; don't forget, *it's the thought that counts!* (However, if you have a Macintosh computer handy, you could make it look pretty fancy pretty easily!) Here are some certificates that were created by Romance Class participants:

⭐ A certificate "For Putting Up With Me Over the Years"
⭐ An award "For Meritorious Conduct in Bed"
⭐ An acknowledgment of "The World's Best Wife"
⭐ A plaque "For Hugs and Kisses Above and Beyond the Call of Duty"

889

✍ Write your own version of Elizabeth Barrett Browning's famous poem . . . "*How do I love thee, let me count the ways . . .*"

✍ Write your own version of "Your Song."

✍ Write new lyrics to any lovesong that strikes your fancy.

890

Learn to do calligraphy. You'll add a touch of class to even the simplest note.

891

➢ Make custom cassette tapes of romantic background music.

➢ Make custom tapes of meaningful, romantic songs as gifts for her.

➢ Make custom tapes of your partner's favorite songs.

➢ Make custom tapes of songs that were hits while you were dating.

892

Make a custom banner to welcome him home from a trip—or just to say "I love you!" Use construction paper, crayons and string; or poster boards, magic markers and twine; or letters individually cut-out and strung along a string!

The root of our problems—all of our problems—is a lack of love.

~ GJPG

Shopping Strategies

893

Always be in a "gift-buying mode." You'll save money in the long run, you'll be prepared, you'll save yourself a hassle, and you'll keep her happy. You've got nothing to lose!

894

Get to know the owner and manager of her favorite dress shop or clothing boutique. Ask them to inform you of new arrivals that they feel your lover will love. (This is an easy way to get surprise gifts that she's guaranteed to appreciate.)

895

Go shopping with no specific task, and no specific goal in mind. *Let the gift find you.*

896

Some people value *objects*—while others value *experiences*. Neither is better than the other: They're just personal preferences. "Object people" see love reflected in things: Flowers, rings, cards, chocolates—*stuff*. It's all a physical manifestation of love. "Experience people" appreciate love in shared experiences: Dinners, romantic weekends, vacations, stolen afternoons, secret rendezvous. It's the loving memories that they value.

897

Catalogs! Send for 'em! Keep 'em in a basket in the bathroom! Scan through 'em occasionally! Note the great gift ideas!

Here are a few catalogs you might find of interest:

- ❦ *The San Francisco Music Box Company* 800-227-2190
- ❦ *The Sharper Image* 800-344-4444
- ❦ *Figi's Gift Catalog* 715-384-6101
- ❦ *The Wine Enthusiast—"Wine as a Lifestyle"* 800-231-0100
- ❦ *Signals* 800-669-9696
- ❦ *The Nature Company* 800-227-1114
- ❦ *The Celebration Fantastic* 800-527-6566
- ❦ *Norm Thompson* 800-547-1160
- ❦ *The Paragon* 800-343-3095
- ❦ *The Music Stand: Gifts from the Performing Arts* 802-295-7044
- ❦ *The J. Peterman Company* 800-231-7341
- ❦ *Taylor Gifts* 610-789-7007
- ❦ *Museum of Fine Arts, Boston* 800-225-5592
- ❦ *Rick's Movie Graphics* 800-669-9999

898

Shopping for an engagement ring? Here are some historical tidbits that will add meaning to the experience:

♦ The ancient Romans believed that diamonds were splinters from falling stars with which Eros' arrows were tipped.

♦ The ancient Greeks believed that diamonds were the tears of the gods.

♦ Because of the brilliance and strength of diamonds, they are viewed as the *ultimate* symbol of love.

899

Try shopping in museum gift shops. They tend to have a unique, classy and/or unusual collection of items:

- ☞ For a touch of class, try art museums.
- ☞ For scientific and technical stuff, try science museums.
- ☞ For spacey stuff, try planetariums.
- ☞ For interesting mementos, try historic museums.
- ☞ For a wide variety of things, try college museums.

These are some of my favorites:

- ✭ *The M.I.T. Shop*, Cambridge, Massachusetts: 617-253-4462
- ✭ *The Hayden Planetarium*, New York City: 212-769-5910
- ✭ *The Smithsonian Institution*, Washington, D.C.: 202-287-3563

900

When window-shopping together, pay close attention for items that she *really likes*. Sneak back later and get them for her. (Store them in your "Gift Closet" for dispersal at your discretion.)

Romance is <u>a state of mind</u>.
It's not so much what you do, as how you do it.

~ GJPG

Romance is <u>a state of being</u>.
It's about taking action on your feelings.

~ GJPG

Travel Tips

901

When you'll be traveling without him, leave him one greeting card for each day you'll be gone.

902

When you'll be traveling for several days without her, leave behind a pile of "I'm Thinking of You" packets.

☞ Get a bunch of large manila envelopes, one for each day you'll be away.

☞ Label each one with a day of the week, and fill each one with *stuff*.

☞ Stuff like: Her favorite candy, poems, little notes, magazines, a photo of you with a funny note, a "Love Coupon" for use when you're back, and an item of lingerie with a note saying "Be wearing this when I return."

903

When she's going away by herself, give her a "Trip Survival Kit." (It would be nice to package it in a gift box or fancy bag—but you don't have to. You can make do with a grocery bag or shoebox labeled with a magic marker.) Anyway . . . now fill the Kit with stuff. (See the item above for a definition of "stuff.")

904

Arrange with an airline steward or stewardess to have a gift or flower delivered to her after the flight is airborne.

905

➤ Pack a card inside his suitcase. Pack 10!

➤ Hide little "love notes" everywhere: In his socks and shoes and shirt pockets and pants pockets and suit pockets and briefcase and suitcase and wallet and notebooks and files and . . .

➤ Pack his favorite candies (any kind that won't melt!)

906

Give him a custom-made tape in a Walkman just before he goes on a business trip. Tell him he can't play it until the plane is airborne.

907

When vacationing together, always take along a couple of little surprise gifts. It's inexpensive, gives you something to look forward to, lets you giftwrap ahead-of-time, and allows you to surprise her at a moment's notice!

908

Mail a card or note to her on the day you leave town, so she'll get it while you're away.

909

Hire a limousine to pick-up your husband at the airport upon his return from a business trip. Send the driver into the terminal to locate and help your husband. Be waiting in the back seat of the limo . . . dressed in your finest lingerie, sipping champagne, and listening to a recording of *Heartstrings*, by Earl Klugh.

910

Sneak off to the airport the night before she's going to leave for a trip. Take one red rose. Rent one of those small storage lockers in the airline terminal. Put the flower in the locker. Sneak back home. Just before she leaves for the airport, hand her the key to the storage locker.

911

Send a greeting card to her hotel, so it's waiting for her when she arrives.

912

Get help from hotel concierges! They're great resources, and they'll get nearly *anything* done for you: From normal things like delivering champagne and a note to his room, to the unusual—like filling his room with 100 balloons . . . or hiding a special gift in the bathtub . . . or whatever outrageous thing you can think up!

913

All kinds of travel tips and current information are available from special newsletters about specific destinations and topics. Here are two:

* *La Belle France: The Sophisticated Guide to France*
  An eight-page monthly newsletter. A yearly subscription is $87.
* *Golf Travel: The Guide for Discriminating Golfers*
  Twelve issues a year at just $79.

Both of these information-packed newsletters are available from Travel Guide Publications. Call 800-225-7825, and in Virginia, 804-295-1200; or write to Post Office Box 3485, Charlottesville, Virginia 22903.

Give It a Twist

914

Start with any basic romantic concept, then *give it a twist*—build on it, expand on it, exaggerate it, use your creativity, put your personal stamp on it—and you'll create an *endless* supply of new romantic ideas.

915

❤ Here are some *twists* on the concept of "Coupons":
  ✯ Coupons made out of your business cards
  ✯ Coupons made on restaurant menus
  ✯ Coupons made on pillow cases
  ✯ Coupons made into bookmarks
  ✯ Coupons inserted into computer documents!
  ✯ Coupons made from magazines
  ✯ Coupons made from lingerie catalogs
  ✯ Coupons made *on* lingerie!

916

❤ A basic romantic concept: *Birthday cards.*
  ☞ Some twists:

  ✶ Send a card a day for a week, a month.
  ✶ Send as many cards as the number of years in his age.
  ✶ Send 25 cards—all on the same day.
  ✶ Hide cards in his briefcase, in the refrigerator.
  ✶ Create your own birthday cards.
     ❦ Make them simple, with crayons or markers.
     ❦ Make them elaborate, created on your computer.
  ✶ Write a birthday greeting on a cake—or on a pizza.
  ✶ Make a poster-sized card.
  ✶ Rent a billboard: Create a **HUGE** birthday card.
  ✶ Write a personal birthday message on a private part of your body . . . and let him discover it.
  ✶ Have them rendered in beautiful *calligraphy.*

917

❤ Basic romantic concepts: *Love letters, love notes, poetry and verses.*
  ☞ Some twists:

  ✝ Write them on nice parchment paper.
  ✝ Turn them into scrolls, tied with ribbon.
  ✝ Frame 'em.
  ✝ Have them rendered in calligraphy.
  ✝ Have your poem set to music.
  ✝ Have the new song recorded.
  ✝ Publish your love letters in a book.
  ✝ Place a love note in the newspaper classified section.
  ✝ Create a poster.
  ✝ Write it up on your computer; add flourishes.
  ✝ Write a letter in code.

918

❤ A basic romantic concept: *Love Coupons.*

☞ Some twists:

    ✯ Start with store-bought "Love Coupons."
       (Good for beginners . . .)

    ✯ Advanced romantics will want to create their *own*
       customized/personalized/wacky/intimate Love Coupons:

        ✳ Backrub coupons
        ✳ Tire-Changing Lesson coupons
        ✳ Music Tape coupons
        ✳ Lovemaking coupons
        ✳ *Joy of Sex* coupons
        ✳ Romantic Dinner (Out) coupons
        ✳ Romantic Dinner (In) coupons
        ✳ Movie (Out) coupons
        ✳ Movie (In, via video) coupons
        ✳ "I'll Do Your Chores" coupons
        ✳ A Ride in the Country coupon
        ✳ A Walk on the Beach coupon
        ✳ Picnic coupons
        ✳ Hot Fudge Sundae coupons
        ✳ Pizza coupons
        ✳ An Evening of Dancing coupon
        ✳ Secret rendezvous coupons
        ✳ A lazy Sunday afternoon coupon
        ✳ A champagne-and-cozy-fire coupon
        ✳ Sleep-in-late coupons
        ✳ Vacation coupons
        ✳ Bed & Breakfast coupons
        ✳ Fantasy coupons
        ✳ "Act out a favorite movie scene" coupon
        ✳ Shopping coupons
        ✳ "Silly celebration" coupons
        ✳ "Sexy Outfit Saturday" coupons
        ✳ Coffee date coupons

919

❤ Some *more* twists:

☞ Love Coupons made from the little slips of paper from Hershey's Kisses. Each coupon is redeemable for one kiss.

☞ "Dollar Bill" Coupons: Make a simply-sketched "one dollar bill"; put your picture in the center; make 100 photocopies; cut 'em out; make a stack. Give them to your lover, along with a list of various activities, and what they'll cost. For example:

⭒ Dinner out: $5
⭒ An *expensive* dinner out: $15
⭒ A movie out: $3
⭒ A movie in: $1
⭒ I'll cook dinner: $12
⭒ I'll bring dinner home: $1
⭒ One backrub: $4
⭒ Going shopping with you: $20
⭒ Making love: $1
⭒ Making love (*when I don't feel like it!*): $98
⭒ Washing your car: $7

920

❤ A basic romantic concept: *"The { _____ }-of-the-Month Clubs"*:

☞ Some twists: Create your own . . .

✓ Beer-of-the-Month Club
✓ Romantic-Restaurant-of-the-Month Club
✓ New-Ice-Cream-Flavor-of-the-Month Club
✓ Lingerie-Outfit-of-the-Month Club
✓ New-Sexual-Position-of-the-Month Club
✓ Stuffed-Animal-of-the-Month Club

Picture This!

921

Have a special photograph blown-up to poster size! If your local photo shop can't do it, the guys at Giganta Photo can! Call them at 212-869-8497, or write to 5 West 46th Street, New York City, New York 10036. Color posters 20-by-30-inches are $32.50.

922

➤ You do, of course, carry a photo of her in your wallet, *don't you?*

➤ And you have an 8-by-10 of her on your desk at work, *right?*?

➤ Do you put funny photos of the two of you on your refrigerator?

923

Turn your drawer-full of miscellaneous photographs and slides into a "Video Photo Album." Your years together will jump back to life as your favorite photos are set to music and blended together into an 8-to-10-minute trip down Memory Lane. All you have to do is gather 60 photos and/or slides, put them in order, choose three favorite songs, and ship 'em off! Scattered Pictures will do the rest. They'll professionally edit the tape, using all kinds of fancy video techniques; they'll add opening and closing titles that you write; and they'll get it back to you in just a few weeks. All this for just $129.95. Call 800-872-0986 or 508-655-2252, or write to Scattered Pictures, 90 Park Avenue, Natick, Massachusetts 01760.

924

Find some old photos of yourself, or go through your photo album. Add funny captions. Mail them to her.

925

Find your old high school yearbook picture. Mail it to her. [If yours is as awful as mine is, it could be the funniest thing you ever give her!]

926

When you're going to be away, tape your photo to your pillow.

Let's Get Physical!

927

Rub "Tiger Balm" on her lower back. Gently. Deeply. Don't wait for her to ask for it, just do it.

928

Talk Dirty To Me: An Intimate Philosophy of Sex, by Sallie Tisdale, is a thought-provoking tome on a subject that embarrasses many people. Tisdale observes that our society is publicly lascivious yet Puritanical at heart. "We're vicariously living out, in a public way, sexual permissiveness— because we don't have one-to-one, intimate, mature conversations about sex." A little "talking dirty" might just be a good thing.

929-930

✦ Take a massage class together. (Get a catalog from your local adult education center.)

✦ Give her a custom made "Love Coupon" good for a professional massage. (Call local health clubs, chiropractor's offices, hotels, or check the Yellow Pages under "Massage.")

931

Go skinny-dipping: In the ocean, in a pond, in a lake, in your pool, in a river, in a creek, in the neighbor's pool!

932

Join the Mile High Club. ✈

933

Make love in other unusual places, too: Cars, trains, beaches, pools, boats, ponds/lakes/oceans, store dressing rooms, libraries, elevators, bathtubs, fire escapes, porches, rooftops, treeforts, boardrooms, saunas, airplanes, kitchen tables and hot tubs.

934

❉ One couple in the Romance Class confided that they have a personal tradition of making love at every wedding reception they attend!

❉ Another couple keeps a U.S. map in their den with pins marking the many places where . . . you guessed it!

For Lovers—Of Books

935

☆ Give her a truckload of books with the word "Love" in their titles:
- ❤ *Love is Letting Go of Fear,* by Gerald Jampolsky
- ❤ *Love,* by Leo Buscaglia
- ❤ *The Art of Loving,* by Erich Fromm
- ❤ *Notes on Love and Courage,* by Hugh Prather
- ❤ *Rediscovering Love,* by Willard Gaylin
- ❤ *The Love Book,* by Karen Casey
- ❤ *The Psychology of Romantic Love,* by Nathaniel Branden
- ❤ *Love Signs,* by Linda Goodman

936

☆ Give him an armload of books with the word "Sex" in their titles:
- ✳ *The Joy of Sex,* by Alex Comfort
- ✳ *Is Sex Necessary?* by James Thurber and E.B. White
- ✳ *The Dieter's Guide to Weight Loss During Sex,* by Richard Smith
- ✳ *Dave Barry's Guide to Marriage and/or Sex*
- ✳ *Sex: If I Didn't Laugh I'd Cry,* by Jess Lair

937

☞ Give him a first edition book by his favorite author.
☞ Give her a book signed by her favorite author.

938

If you need help finding a special book, call Ms. Jeryl Metz, a professional "book tracker"! She's got an encyclopedic brain, and remembers every book she's ever seen or heard about. (She specializes in children's books; tracks other topics, too; but not sexual/erotic titles.) Call her at 212-864-3055, or fax to 212-222-8048, or write to 697 West End Avenue, 13A, New York City, New York 10025.

939

Write your *own* book!

* A love story (non-fiction)—about the two of you.
* A "Romance" novel—based loosely on the two of you.
* A mystery, a science fiction saga, a Western.
* A picture-book—with photos or sketches of your life together.
* You *could* actually publish your book! (See #395)

🄑🄑🄑🄑🄑🄑🄑🄑🄑🄑

What is the speed of love?

~ GJPG

🄑🄑🄑🄑🄑🄑🄑🄑🄑🄑

940

If he already has that special book in hand, and you'd like to make it even *more* special, you could have it bound in leather for him. Paperbacks can be made to look like family heirlooms, and old, ratty books can be beautifully restored. Call the Argosy Bookstore at 212-753-4455, or drop-in at 116 East 59th Street, New York City 10022.

941

One of the best used bookstores anywhere is the Avenue Victor Hugo Bookstore, in Boston. In addition to thousands of books, they stock more than a quarter million old magazines! They specialize in fiction, science fiction, rare books and first editions. They'll conduct free searches through their inventory upon request, and they ship books and magazines anywhere for you. Call them at 617-266-7746.

942

The largest used book center *in the world* is in the village of Hay-On-Wye, an ancient market town just over the Welsh/English border. It boasts more than a *million* books, on 11 miles of shelving. A variety of shops specialize in everything from children's books to cookbooks, and from poetry to textbooks. One store carries nothing but first editions of Dickens!

Planning doesn't destroy spontaneity... it creates opportunity.

For the Forgetful

943

On the first day of every month, review your calendar and plan some romantic activities.

944

Get professional help! No, no, I don't mean a psychiatrist—hire a *personal shopper.* He or she can help you run those errands and pick-up those gifts that you always seem to forget about.

945

- Review the chapter called "Memorize This List!"—which helps you create a detailed and customized list of your lover's favorite things. Now, write a list of 10 romantic gifts you could buy, or gestures you could perform, based on those favorite things.
- Keep the list in your briefcase or appointment calendar, or on the refrigerator or nightstand.

946

Which 10 ideas in this book do you think your lover would love most? Don't simply jot them down somewhere—write them directly into your appointment calendar, and schedule time to perform the gestures or buy the gifts. [Hey, don't wait till later—do it right now! Yes, I'm talkin' to *you*!]

947

Buy some small, red, heart-shaped ❤ stickers and place one on the face of your wristwatch. It's a reminder to think of your lover every time you check the time. If you're like most of us, that's about a *thousand* times a day! ❤

948

✭ Keep a list of toll-free 800 numbers handy—they're a great source of information and romantic possibilities.

✭ Keep this book handy—don't stick it up on your bookshelf!! Carry it around in your briefcase. Keep it where you do your reading: The family room—the bathroom?! Keep it next to the *TV Guide*. Skim through it weekly. Make it a handy resource.

949

Ask your friendly local florist to call you once every month—as a reminder that you oughta be bringin' home some flowers to your honey!

950

Get a free one-year subscription to a unique publication from yours truly: *The LoveLetter*™—*The Newsletter of Romantic Ideas*. It's a $25 value, and it's full of creative, unusual and wonderful ideas, gifts and gestures. Just send your name and address to:

LoveLetter
P.O. Box 226
Weymouth, Massachusetts
02188-0001

Sign-up yourself, your spouse, your boyfriend/girlfriend, your brother, your parents, your friends—anyone who needs a good swift kick-in-the-pants, or who would appreciate receiving lots of great romantic ideas on a regular basis!

Cars

951

Put a love note or poem under the driver's side windshield wiper of his car. (Don't forget that true romantics let *nothing* stand in their way . . . If it's raining or snowing—put the note in a zip-lock plastic bag!)

952

Other items to put under the windshield wiper:

- A single rose
- A candy bar
- Wildflowers
- A little book
- A poem
- A pizza coupon
- A cartoon
- A Love Coupon
- A short note

953

Wash and vacuum her car until it sparkles like new.

954

Hang a pair of your panties on his rear-view mirror. [No pun intended.]

955

Hide little one-line notes all over his car: On the sun visor, in the glove compartment, in the ash tray, in the trunk, under the hood, on the mirror, on the seat belt . . .

956

Fill her glove compartment with **m&m**'s. Or jelly beans. Or bubble gum. Or Fire Balls. Or Hershey's Kisses. Or Lifesavers.

957

Fill the back seat of your car with pillows. Go for a little drive. Use your imagination.

958

When's the last time you went out "parking"?!? [FYI, I checked all the Rule Books, and discovered that there's no upper age limit for playing this sport . . . All you need is a valid driver's license.]

959

Make a cassette tape of romantic songs. Stick it in the tape player of her car, and set it up to play when she turns the ignition on.

960

Buying a new (or new-used) car? Arrange to have it delivered one day earlier than she expects it, park it in the driveway, and tie it with a giant red bow!

961

Drive by his parking lot at work. Attach balloons to the side mirror. Tape streamers to the back windshield. Leave a sealed love note on the front seat.

962

Surprise her with a personalized license plate!

☞ Most states charge somewhere between $50 and $100 a year.

☞ Many of the most popular and common names and phrases are already taken, so you'll have to use a little creativity. Consider these possibilities, and use them to spark your own ideas:

- ✯ Her initials
- ✯ Both of your initials
- ✯ Her birthdate
- ✯ Your anniversary date
- ✯ Her height
- ✯ Your pet name for her

- ✯ "Code phrases"
  - ➤ ILY
  - ➤ 14U2NV
  - ➤ 4EVER
  - ➤ UNME
  - ➤ IMWLD4U

☞ Note: The most populous states usually have the most digits in their license plates, giving the creative copywriter more flexibility. (One innovative man in the Romance Class registered his wife's car in a neighboring state [New York] so he could use *seven* digits to spell-out his wife's name.)

*The anticipation
is often just as much fun as the event
or gift itself.*

~ GJPG

963

Write and design a fake traffic ticket; place it under the windshield wiper.

➤ Possible violations include:
  * ✳ Leaving the scene of a love affair
  * ✳ Speeding down the highway of life
  * ✳ Driving me crazy

➤ Possible options for making restitution include:
  * ✳ Taking the judge out to dinner
  * ✳ Bribing the officer with sexual favors
  * ✳ One sensual backrub

964

Fill his car with balloons.

Sports

965

You can put your sports fan on a baseball card! Former New York Yankee pitcher Jim Bouton runs a shop called Big League Cards. Send 'em a photo, some cleverly-written "statistics" and $39 (plus $5 for shipping), and they'll send you 50 cards! Call 201-907-0700.

966

Looking for sports memorabilia? The place to go is The Collector's Stadium, at 214 Sullivan Street, in New York City. They have *thousands* of items, from caps and T-shirts to balls and bats and signed autographs and photos and posters etc. Call 212-353-1531.

967

➤ Visit the Sports Museum of New England, home of the "Larry Bird Statue" and the "Bobby Orr Statue." They also house tons o' stuff from a wide variety of sports, in addition to memorabilia, videos and displays on the Red Sox, Celtics, Bruins and Patriots. Call 'em at 617-621-0520, or visit the museum in East Cambridge, Massachusetts, just across the Charles River from Boston.

➤ If your lover loves *cars*, take him to the Indianapolis Motor Speedway Hall of Fame Museum. It contains one of the world's largest and most varied collections of racing cars. The museum regularly rotates the 200 racing and antique passenger cars in and out of its multi-million-dollar collection, with about 75 on display at any one time. Visit them at 4790 West 16th Street, Indianapolis, or call 317-484-6747.

"OKAY, LORETTA, I'LL SHARE MY FEELINGS··· I WANT TO WATCH THE BALLGAME."

968

While he's watching sports on TV, bring him peanuts and popcorn, beer and ice-cream bars. When it comes to sports fanatics, the only reasonable philosophy to adopt is "If you can't beat 'em, join 'em!"

969

Find a sport you can enjoy *together*. It doesn't matter if it's a spectator sport or a participatory one—just so the two of you truly enjoy it together.

○ Polo or Ping Pong? Championship Thoroughbred Racing or Championship Wrestling? Football or Frisbee? Baseball or Bridge?

○ Note: If your guy has an extremely competitive nature, stay away from participatory sports where you play each other one-on-one. (A little romance can't compete against a maniac on a tennis court!)

Great Escapes

970

Visit Liverpool, England, for a "Magical Mystery Tour" of The Beatles' hometown. Walk down Penny Lane, see the Cavern Club, visit the multimedia exhibit, and ponder the Eleanor Rigby statue (dedicated to "All the lonely people.") And, of course, there's The Beatles Shop, which is chockfull of memorabilia and music.

971

To book a vacation on an "Impossibly Romantic Island," call Ralph Locke, who personally handles bookings for Young Island, St. Vincent, in the Grenadines. Young Island has a 60-guest maximum, white sand beaches, tennis courts and cozy cottages spread out on 35 acres of paradise. Depending on whether or not you want to spend additional nights on their luxury yacht, prices range from $2,065 to $3,395 per couple per week. Call Ralph at 800-223-1108.

972-978

➤ Great Escape #1: Weekending in Bermuda, Catalina or Tahoe.

➤ Great Escape #2: Skiing Vail or Killington in the middle of the week.

➤ Great Escape #3: Trekking in Peru, Nepal or Scotland!

➤ Great Escape #4: Shooting the rapids in Colorado.

➤ Great Escape #5: A second honeymoon in the Poconos!

➤ Great Escape #6: A *third* honeymoon in Hawaii!

➤ Great Escape #7: A *fourth* honeymoon at Niagara Falls!

Romance expresses love.
Love creates intimacy.
Intimacy enhances trust.
Trust builds commitment.
Commitment is the cornerstone of monogamy.
Monogamy flourishes amid romance.

~ GJPG

979

The romance of the open road . . . the vacation that never ends . . . the RV lifestyle! (Some people think that "RV" stands for "Recreational Vehicle." *I* say it stands for "Romantic Vehicle.") I'll tell you from personal experience that many of my most romantic experiences with Tracey have been aboard our **Holiday Rambler RV.** We've visited many romantic locales without leaving behind the comforts of home. (We even have a double shower head installed so we can . . . well, use your imagination!) We save money, we go where we please, and we enjoy the company of RV enthusiasts—who are among the friendliest people on earth. If you think RVs are just for retirees, think again!

- ➽ 800-327-7778 . . . will get you CruiseAmerica, which rents all makes and sizes of RVs—so you can try different units before buying one.
- ➽ 800-543-3622 . . . will put you in contact with the Family Motor Coach Association.
- ➽ 800-245-4778 . . will put you in touch with my friends at **Holiday Rambler,** which makes the best RVs on the road!

980

For a "New Age" escape, visit Sedona, Arizona. Visit the energy vortices, participate in fire-walking, meditate, and visit the shops. Call the Sedona Chamber of Commerce at 602-282-7722.

More Miscellany

981

Musical greeting cards! Yes, open one up and it plays an electronic tune for you! Look in fine card shops and gift shops.

982

A gift-a-day for the 12 Days of Christmas! (Note: You begin 12 days *before* Christmas.)

983

Create a "Count-Down Calendar" to mark the time remaining until a birthday, wedding, anniversary, vacation or "Mystery Day."

984

* Loosen your purse strings.
* Loosen your schedule.
* Loosen your *attitude.*

985

Everyone should, at one time or another in his or her life:

✦ Go skinny-dipping; go gambling in Las Vegas; take a moonlit stroll on a beach in the Caribbean; sing silly love songs to one another; get giddy on champagne; stay up all night talking and making love and talking and making love and eating and making love and watching old movies and making love and making love.

༜༜༜༜༜༜༜༜༜༜༜༜༜༜

Practice "Couple Thinking":
View yourself as a member of a couple first.
Think of "us" and "we" before "me" and "I."

- GJPG

༜༜༜༜༜༜༜༜༜༜༜༜༜༜

986

Is he full of hot air? Is she an air-head? Then visit one of America's many *hot air balloon festivals!*

✤ The U.S. National Hot Air Balloon Festival: Early August, in Indianola, Iowa. Call 515-961-8415.

✤ The "Greit Oktoberfest Balloon Rallye": Late August/early September, in Dansville, New York. Call 716-335-3708.

✤ The U.S. Hot Air Balloon Nat'l. Championships: Late July/ August, in Baton Rouge, Louisiana. Call 800-527-6843 or 504-752-1079.

✤ The International Balloon Fiesta: Mid-October, in Albuquerque, New Mexico. Call 800-284-2282.

OutRAGEous!!!!!!!!!

987

THINK BIG! That's not just a PHILOSOPHY, it's the name of a truly OUTRAGEOUS operation that sells GIANT STUFF. Stuff like six-foot CRAYOLA CRAYONS, oversized BASEBALLS, giant safety pins, PAPER CLIPS, humongous light bulbs, note pads and kitchen utensils! The romantic possibilities are staggering! Call THINK BIG! for their incredible catalog, at 800-487-4244, or write to 960 Brook Road, Conshohocken, Pennsylvania 19428. Or visit their two showrooms: East coast: 390 West Broadway, New York, New York 10012; West coast: 1000-176 Universal Center Drive, Universal City, California 91608.

988
"The Grand Gesture"

The once-in-a-lifetime event. The surprise three-week vacation to Hawaii. The month-long trek through the Himalayas. The new red Porsche.

Wouldn't it be a shame to look back on your life and not be able to say that you did one *incredible, unbelievable, outrageous and wonderful thing* for and with your lover?

❋ One bold husband in the Romance Class went out and *replaced his wife's entire wardrobe* instead of going on vacation one year! "It cost me $7,500, but it was worth it!" he exclaimed.

❋ One woman, whose husband is a partner in a prestigious law firm, arranged a *surprise three-week vacation tour of Europe's vineyards* for her husband. He nearly had a heart attack when he realized that his flight to Chicago was really a flight to Paris, that his wife was on board the flight, and that all his work was being taken care of by another partner. His wife reports that he *did* finally calm down and had the time of his life.

989

Greet him at the front door wearing your wedding gown.

❧❧❧❧❧❧❧❧❧❧❧❧❧❧❧

The "Battle of the Sexes" is a foolish concept.
Just think about it . . . If one side won
the war, what would we do, take
the opposite sex prisoner?!

~ GJPG

❧❧❧❧❧❧❧❧❧❧❧❧❧❧❧

990

∾ Surprise vacations!
∾ Kidnappings!
∾ Making love in an elevator!
∾ Renting a billboard.

991

Do the impossible. Get Superbowl tickets; find that out-of-print book; meet her at the airport when she *knows* you're tied-up and can't make it; get Yankee/Lakers/Vikings/Bruins playoff tickets; cook a meal; get tickets to a sold-out show.

This Could Become Habit-Forming

992

Read an inspirational passage every morning and evening.

✦ Suggestions for inspirational readings:

 ✹ *The Prophet*, by Kahlil Gibran
 ✹ *The Bible*, by You-Know-Who
 ✹ *A Course In Miracles*, Foundation For Inner Peace
 ✹ *The Quiet Answer*, by Hugh Prather

993

Create a "Love Fund." Deposit one dollar into a jar every time you make love. [There's nothing like a little positive reinforcement!]

994

Finding special meaning in various items is a fun habit to develop. Here are a few album titles that might inspire you . . . Attach notes to an album, cassette or CD, and give it to your lover. Create a musical "Love Coupon" with a theme that matches the title of the album. (You may not like Madonna, but you may want to use her album titled *True Blue* to express that you are.)

- ✹ *A Night to Remember,* Cyndi Lauper
- ✹ *Anticipation,* Carly Simon
- ✹ *August,* Eric Clapton
- ✹ *Captured Angel,* Dan Fogelberg
- ✹ *Desire,* Bob Dylan
- ✹ *Fantasy,* Carole King
- ✹ *Girls Just Wanna Have Fun,* Cyndi Lauper
- ✹ *I'm Your Baby Tonight,* Whitney Houston
- ✹ *In the Dark,* The Grateful Dead
- ✹ *Lawyers in Love,* Jackson Browne
- ✹ *One Night of Sin,* Joe Cocker
- ✹ *Spend the Night,* The Isley Brothers
- ✹ *Still Crazy After All These Years,* Paul Simon
- ✹ *True Blue,* Madonna
- ✹ *Give and Take,* Eric Tingstat & Nancy Rumbel
- ✹ *Romance (Music for Piano),* on the Narada Label
- ✹ *Beauty of Love,* Shardad
- ✹ *Euphoria,* Ottmar Liebert & Luna Negra

995

♥ Make a habit of using this book to enhance your love life! Circle ideas you know (or suspect) your lover will love.

> ➤ When trying these ideas, don't just follow my suggestions blindly—personalize them, make them your own, put your own unique stamp on them! Don't do anything that doesn't "fit" for you. Find something that *does* fit—and then go wild!

♥ Use this book as a kick-in-the-pants to your wonderful but negligent lover. Circle the items that turn you on, then give the book to him along with a note saying: "Here's the biggest (and last) hint you'll get from me!"

996

Capture your memories and the good times . . . Or, as they say at Kodak, "For the times of your life"—take up photography! Whether you use a sophisticated 35mm or a Polaroid, it'll add fun to your outings, and provide you with scrapbooks full of good memories.

997

Get into the habit of bringing flowers home once a week.

998

Capture your memories and the good times... Keep a journal. It will benefit you in lots of ways. Many Romance Class participants have observed that creative ideas often flow while they're writing in their journals.

999

To help you create a soundtrack to your own personal love affair: Bring home some new music once a month.

- ❧ **January:** *Power of Love*, Luther Vandross
- ❧ **February:** *Time, Love & Tenderness*, Michael Bolton
- ❧ **March:** *Forever Friends*, Justo Almario
- ❧ **April:** *Down To The Moon*, Andreas Vollenweider
- ❧ **May:** *Lifestyle (Living & Loving)*, John Klemmer
- ❧ **June:** *Livin' Inside Your Love*, George Benson
- ❧ **July:** *Sun Singer*, Paul Winter
- ❧ **August:** *Summer*, George Winston
- ❧ **September:** *Heartstrings*, Earl Klugh
- ❧ **October:** *Openings*, William Ellwood
- ❧ **November:** *She Describes Infinity*, Scott Cossu
- ❧ **December:** *Something of Time*, Nightnoise

〰〰〰〰〰〰〰〰〰〰〰

Yes, we live in a modern, sophisticated age—
but we still feel ancient, primal emotions.

~ GJPG

〰〰〰〰〰〰〰〰〰〰〰

1000 + 1

1000

Best and Worst Gifts:

- ❤ **Best:** The gift of time.
- ♣ **Worst:** Meaningless gifts.

1001

Enjoy yourself

Express yourself

REVEAL YOURSELF

Share yourself

Know thyself

Love yourself

DEVELOP YOURSELF

Risk yourself

Be YOuRself

Give yourself!

*Romance is a recognition that
love in the abstract has no real meaning at all.*

~ GJPG

Introduction to "LoveStories"

∞

The inspirational, funny, outrageous and touching stories in this next section are all true. This is a small but representative sampling of the hundreds of stories that I've been privileged to hear. I've gathered these stories throughout the last 15 years of teaching the Romance Class. Many have come from conversations; some have come from people sharing their stories on radio call-in shows; and many have come from the letters people send to me. ∼ I am constantly impressed with people's generosity in sharing their experiences, in the hope of helping others. I am also delighted with people's creativity in expressing their love for one another. I find you folks an endless source of inspiration. My heartfelt thanks to all of you. ∼ And to everyone, thanks for opening your hearts to the message of love conveyed by your fellow romantics.

— Gregory J.P. Godek

A Military Romance

∞

Who says "Real Men" aren't romantic? **My husband is very romantic, and he's a MARINE!** ∼ After we spent our first week together, Tom had to go back to his duty station—800 miles away! I gave him my favorite stuffed animal—a dolphin—to keep him company. ∼ Well, that dolphin has been to 13 countries after 4 years of marriage! **I'd sneak it into his backpack** or duffle bag whenever he'd deploy. He'd send me photos of the dolphin on his bunk on the ship off of Somalia; in a tent in the freezing winter of Norway, and on the streets of Bubai! ∼ Now our daughter Emily plays with that same well-traveled dolphin. We'll catch ourselves watching her with it, and tears well up in our eyes. ∼ **Oh, here's another idea** that I had while Tom was deployed and I was pregnant: During my monthly doctor appointments I would tape record the baby's heartbeat, and send Tom the tape. I would also record messages from me. Tom says he cried every time he heard that little heartbeat! ∼ Here's to the Marines—The few. The proud. The *romantic!*

- K.K.R., NORTH CAROLINA

A Christmas Proposal

∞

When Barbara walked into Santa's Village on December 18th with her girlfriend, Stephanie, she thought she would be surprising me with a photo of her on Santa's lap. I had been bugging her for such a photo for weeks . . . but little did she know that it would be she who would receive the big surprise! ⌁ **My original plan was simply to dress up in a tuxedo,** and pop out from behind the scenery of Santa's Workshop. But that morning, as I watched the Laurel & Hardy classic, March of the Toy Soldier, true inspiration struck! I made a few frantic phone calls, then rushed over to the only costume shop I could find that had a palace guard outfit in stock. When I told the clerks my new idea they eagerly assisted. They even helped add the finishing touch: heavy make-up that really made me look like a toy soldier. With a white face, bright red cheeks, and a wide moustache, my costume was complete. **It looked so good that I hardly recognized myself in the shop mirror.** ⌁ I had asked a friend, Mike, to videotape my proposal, so he was already there (pretending to tape his children's visit with Santa) when I arrived. I placed myself "at attention" next to Santa, and within minutes Barb and Stephanie arrived. ⌁ But instead of approaching Santa immediately, they dawdled, perusing the ornaments and joking with the elf workers. I was dying! My costume was thick and itchy, and I began to feel beads of sweat trickling down my forehead and upper lip. After watching several children sit on Santa's lap and recite long lists of the toys they wanted for Christmas, I considered marching down and dragging Barb to Santa myself! But she finally approached Santa's throne. She glanced in my direction, didn't recognize me, and sat on Santa's lap. ∽ He asked, **"Have you been a good girl this year?"** ∽ "Oh, yes!" ∽ "And what would you like for Christmas?" ∽ I held my breath. I leaned over to hear her whisper, "My engagement ring." ∽ I couldn't have hoped for a better moment! ∽ Although I was shaking with nervous excitement, **I got down on one knee** and gently touched Barb's arm. She turned and looked at me, perplexed. As far as she knew, I was just some kid dressed up in a toy soldier outfit. But as I began to talk she slowly realized who this was. She went from merely perplexed to completely surprised. ∽ Frankly, I can't remember exactly what I said—and the video failed to catch all the words—but it did catch my trembling hands pulling out the engagement ring, and Barb's elated expression. ∽ We were married the following October 22nd.

~ S. & B. J., CALIFORNIA

"I Love My Wife"

∞

One day about five years ago my husband came home and sat in the driveway, beeping his horn. "What's going on?" I wondered, curious and slightly irritated. I ran out and stood staring. **My irritation turned to surprise and delight.** Painted along the side of his 1970 Ford pickup in one-foot red letters was "I LOVE MY WIFE". ∽ This message was repeated on the other side and along the tailgate, too. As if that weren't enough, on the hood he'd painted a big red heart (with a Cupid's arrow through it) with "Jim & Barbara" written on it. And then, on the inside, there was another red heart: upholstered on the backrest of the seat! ∽ All of this was applied quite permanently, and my husband has been driving this pickup around for years. Actually, some of it is fading a little—and he plans to get it freshened-up soon. ∽ Needless to say, **we won a "Most Romantic Story" contest** in a local magazine, and made the front page of the newspaper on Valentine's Day. ∽ And *now* . . . this same wonderful romantic guy is working on a surprise for me for our upcoming 25th anniversary on August 2nd. The interesting thing is, he started working on it last August 3rd! He's been busy every week since then running around doing things in preparation. He tells me it involves just the two of us—so it's not a big party. He tells me he's not building something. I'm stumped! ∿ He's starting to panic now because he says he's running out of time; there's only five months left! He's keeping **a journal of all the funny things that have happened along the way** to share with me. I think his new romantic surprise is as crazy as his painted truck idea because he says that people who hear what he's doing simply don't believe him at first ∿ I can't wait!! ∿ By the way, my romantic guy and I have five children. And for as much as we love them, we have always made time for each other. My motto is: **Be a wife first and a mother second.** It works for me! ∿ I have my crazy and creative moments, too. A couple years ago I created a special calendar for my husband: it featured boudoir photographs of me. One of the photos is of *me,* standing naked in the back of the "I LOVE MY WIFE" pickup truck. Of *course* it was tastefully done! In fact, my husband has some of the photos tacked to his bulletin board at work!

~ B. & J. K., CALIFORNIA

Surprise!

It was Valentine's Day, 1989. My boyfriend had invited me to his place for breakfast. ✑ I arrived to find the kitchen table in the living room, in front of the fireplace. It was set with flowers, candles, a delicious breakfast and champagne glasses filled with ginger ale. ✑ Although this was a wonderfully romantic setting, **I began to sense that my boyfriend was somehow uncomfortable.** I waited a while, and finally asked him if anything was wrong. ✑ He looked at me kind of funny. Then he stood up and told me he had something for me. He reached down, unzipped his pants, and revealed . . . a heart-shaped note with "I Love You" written in orange crayon! The note was tied to his *you-know-what* with a *burlap* string. No *wonder* he'd looked uncomfortable! He'd had it tied there all morning. ✑ To this day I have that heart tied—with the burlap string—to the trunk of a stuffed elephant he gave me.

~ A.L., British Columbia, Canada

A Wedding Count-Down

∞

I'm convinced that during our engagement, my fiancé, Mark, consulted with you in secret (although he adamantly denies it!) For the year leading up to our wedding day he marked our monthly "Negative Anniversary" with a special gift denoting the number of months until our big day. ∼ At T-minus 11 months: I thought he'd given me a dozen roses, until he pointed out that there were 11 roses—one for each month until our wedding day, October 9th, 1993. On the ninth of each month to follow he gave me: **10** chocolates (for his "sweetie"!) ∼ **9** m&ms (my favorites.) ∼ **8** wedding bell balloons (self-explanatory!) ∼ **7** lottery tickets (I won $7! Lucky 7!) ∼ **6** red roses (delivered to my hairdresser's salon—much to the delight of the staff and other customers, as well as myself!) ∼ **5** dice (for "taking a chance" on him.) ∼ **4** ten-dollar Victoria's Secret gift certificates (self-explanatory!) ∼ **3** stargazer lilies (our wedding theme flowers.) ∼ **2** "Goofy" slippers (a nickname we call each other.) ∼ **1** heart balloon (until he gave me his *real heart* one month later!) Now, years later, Mark continues to make frequent romantic gestures . . . so I know that he did NOT consult with you during our engagement—he did it on his own!

~ K.&M.S., V<small>IRGINIA</small>

A Romantic Resumé

∞

Dear Miss H.:

For the past several years I have been attempting to be the person that you have wanted me to be. And over those years I have been trying to be that person, with little or no success.

Once again I am applying for the position of your one and only true love. I have many qualifications that will allow me to succeed in this position on a permanent basis.

My salary requirements include unconditional forgiveness for any past mistakes that I have made, and your total commitment to our relationship.

I have enclosed a copy of my resumé for your consideration. Please review it carefully when considering me for this position. Once again, thank you for your time. I look forward to your prompt reply.

Yours Always, Love,

D.E.V.

~ D.E.V., Oнio

Resumé

Objective:

To obtain the position of your one and only partner for life. This includes being best friends always.

Education:

Reading *1001 Ways To Be Romantic,* as well as 8 years of being your friend.

Career Summary:

12 years of dating other people and determining that you are the one person that I LOVE the most and wish to make happy for the rest of my life.

Employment:

1984- present: Miss H.
Part-time boyfriend/best friend. Responsibilities include listening, being there when needed, caring, loving, sharing, communicating, having the same interests and sharing the same values.

1965-1984: Adolescence
Growing up to be an adult. Watching my mother and father maintain a healthy relationship, raising four wonderful children, learning right from wrong, and respect for others.

Prior: Family History
Warm, generous family. Traits handed down from the distant past.

Hobbies:

Boating, flying, walking, bicycling, holding hands, kissing, hugging, #%&*@$#%^#, and being there when needed.

References:

Furnished upon request.

Menu Madness

∞

My boyfriend, Paul, had taken me out to dinner at a restaurant we'd never visited before. After we were seated, our waiter informed us that the restaurant had an "initiation ritual" for first time customers. **I thought this was a little odd,** but since Paul and I are both a little wild and crazy, we figured we'd go along. ∽ The waiter handed us a menu-like booklet. The first page gave us the background of the restaurant and the chef named "Sparky," who had devised a game for couples to have fun while waiting for their meals. ∽ I thought to myself, this is insane; but I kept it to myself and read on. ∽ We were directed to complete a task on each of seven pages of the booklet. **The first task was to give my partner a kiss** or hug. Just for good measure I gave him both. The second task was to balance a spoon on our noses. While attempting this feat I couldn't help but wonder if other people were watching us. Oh well. ∽ The third task was for my partner to eat three slices of lemon and whistle "Rudolph the Red-Nose Reindeer." What a laugh! The fourth task directed us to eat 30 grapes—and after every fifth grape to say a phrase three times to your partner, such as "I love you." The fifth task asked us to search our memories and "remember that very special first kiss." We had different recollections! The sixth task was to tell one another why we care for and love each other. **Now this was getting serious,** and I was getting a little emotional. So was Paul. Now I thought, this isn't such a bad game after all! ∽ On to the final task, Number Seven. I was instructed to take my time with this one, because the last task "requires a deep sense of commitment." I turned the page to read these words: ∽ "Elizabeth, I cannot spend another day of my life without knowing that we will spend the rest of our lives together. WILL YOU MARRY ME? Love, Paul" ∽ He then reached into his pocket and handed me a beautiful diamond ring, while saying aloud the same words, "Will you marry me?"

- E.G. Ohio

Love In The News

I wanted to do something special for my boyfriend on Valentine's day. Inspiration struck when I combined two facts: first, that Kory is a life-style editor at our local newspaper, *The Evening News;* and second, I'd recently taken an art class at college, and had piles of large newsprint paper for sketching. ∼ **I decided to create a special newspaper** for Kory. Instead of The Evening News, mine was called *The Loving News.* ∼ I folded the paper into the same size and shape as an actual newspaper. I re-created the layout and graphic look of *The Evening News.* ∼ I wrote a front page story on our relationship. I had a Sports Page with an article about Kory's favorite basketball player, Chris Mullin (and how Chris owed his career to Kory!) I wrote poems for the Poetry Corner; made a crossword puzzle; and wrote several other columns that pertained to us, our relationship, our lives, and our love. I put a lot of humor into it **so he wouldn't think it was too "mushy."** ∼ The project took several days to complete—but it was worth seeing the amazed look on Kory's face.

~ L.R., INDIANA

Boudoir Photography

W hat comes to mind when you think of "Boudoir Photography"? A woman in a sexy-yet-demure-pose, dressed in elegant lingerie, photographed in soft focus? Well, I'd like to expand your horizons and introduce you to "Boudoir Photography for Men"! **I was looking for something special and unusual and customized** to do for my wife. It took a number of phone calls for me to find the right person. When I finally did, I told him he had carte blanche with his ideas for the photos. ∿ **We met secretly** for several photo sessions over a period of two months. We took photos outside and in; we took casual shots and posed shots; we took photos of me fully clothed and, well . . . use your imagination! ∿ We then took the best 12 photos and created a wall calendar. My wife calls it her "GQ Calendar of her very own male model." I'm very flattered because, believe me, the only thing "GQ" about me is my big toe. But my wife knew that 13 years ago when she married me. ∿ I've come to appreciate that the best gift is the gift of myself and my time. (And an occasional sexy photo doesn't hurt!)

— R.H., FLORIDA

First Kiss

∞

During my junior year at college we had a "Secret Santa" gift exchange. In the random drawing of names of people living in our house, Alan got my name. (At the time I didn't know that Alan had taped my name to the bottom of the cup, so that he would definitely end up with me! I suspected nothing.) ∿ Two months later, just after Valentine's Day, I received a chocolate rose in my mailbox. **Attached was a "Secret Admirer" note.** Two more followed. I soon confronted Alan via e-mail, asking if he was my Secret Admirer. He confessed. Meanwhile, a real rose was waiting for me. ∿ Soon after that Alan asked me to help him with some theater staging. He's in charge of the lighting design for all the shows at the university. We'd collaborated previously, as I handle the music direction. **Only this time, there was a twist to the scene** . . . ∿ Alan asked me to stand in the center of the stage while he tried some different background and lighting combinations. Then he displayed different scenes on the screen behind me. He said that each one showed a place that he'd considered as **the setting for our first kiss.** I froze in anticipation! He showed a forest. A city skyline at sunset. A beach

∞

scene. A starry sky. Then he said that he'd finally realized that the location wasn't important. The screen went blank; and soft, **romantic blue lighting came on.** And . . . It's a year-and-a-half later, and we're engaged.

‹ L.I., New Jersey

Catching a Mermaid

∞

My favorite episodes involving romance, of recent years, have taken place when I was working on the Greek islands. The backdrop itself creates an atmosphere where anything seems possible. ⮑ On my days off, I snorkel, free dive and spear fish. One of the most romantic days of my life began when my eyes met those of a beautiful Italian woman, while on the water taxi which was taking tourists to a beach reachable only by boat. (A romantic concept in itself, don't you think?!) **Our eyes met through the goggles I was wearing.** I also wore huge fins, and carried a large knife and spear gun. Lord only knows what she first thought of me! But the water beckoned me, and I dove off the stern, in search of fish. **Little did I know that I was about to catch a mermaid.** ⮑ About 20 minutes later I was about half a mile off shore and 20 feet down, when a big fish flashed by me. I got off a lucky shot. I broke the surface with a splash, a yell, and a fish struggling on the end of the trident. (I do this for my own sense of drama.) I suddenly noticed the woman from the boat treading water about 10 yards away, watching me and enjoying the show. I couldn't have asked for a better entrance.

I started to introduce myself (trying not to be distracted, as she looked like a goddess in the buff), **only to discover that she spoke only Italian.** I speak Greek, English, a little French and Spanish—but no Italian. ∼ Did this stop us? Not at all. We made a dinner date for later that night at the only Italian restaurant on the island. ∼ I must confess that one of my little romantic secrets is to become friends with restaurant owners. I met with this particular owner, planned some surprises, pre-paid the bill, and . . . later that night **we were serenaded by the violinist** and the accordion player; our table was strewn with rose petals; and the waiters made sure that my lovely woman's wine glass was never less than one sip away from empty. ∼ The best part was when I asked for the bill. The waiter acted insulted, and insisted that the restaurant would not charge me. When I demanded to know why, he explained—in both Greek and Italian—that it was because we were "a beautiful, beautiful couple! And there are times when Love herself is in the restaurant—and it would be hubris to be associated with the vulagrity of money!"

- A.M., Maine, USA/Greece

"Holy romance, Batman!"

How and why does romantic inspiration strike? I don't know. But I *do* know that I appreciate it when it strikes my husband! He did something for me that was so amazing that **I still shake my head in wonderment.** I hesitate slightly to share it with you because it is . . . unusual . . . not your standard dozen-roses-kind-of-gesture. ∼ I had just returned from a trip to England with 39 students (that's *another* story!) and was simply appreciating being back with my husband. During our first evening back together I noticed a bandage on his thigh. Concerned, I asked him what had happened. He didn't say a word. He simply peeled off the bandage to reveal—a tattoo of a bat! Now, at this point, you need to know two things. First, I *love* bats. And second, my husband is *not* a tattoo sort of person. He's a college English professor **who's never done anything remotely like this in his life.** Needless to say, the bat was a huge and very appreciated surprise. ∼ I've since reciprocated—with temporary tattoos. (Sorry, no needles for me!) Plus, temporary tattoos are quite versatile!

— C.M., ALABAMA

Dinner Plans

∞

We had plans to go out for dinner. Nothing unusual, right? Wrong! ⁓ I'd gotten ready early, so that while my girlfriend was showering, I . . . 1 Quickly uncovered the fireplace and lit the wood that I had pre-stacked. 2 Set-up a folding table in front of the fireplace. 3 Covered the table with a nice tablecloth, and set it with wine, two crystal glasses, a single red rose and one candle. 4 Heated-up the full-course dinner that I had prepared beforehand! ⁓ By the time she had finished showering, putting on her make-up, and getting dressed, I was calmly waiting for her at the dinner table. Her look of surprise was priceless! And the memory we created is timeless.

~ J.M., WASHINGTON

"Rhino-Love"

∞

I have been dating my now fiancée for three years. During the first few months of our relationship I started a strange ritual of butting her with the top of my head, pretending to be a rhinoceros. **I borrowed this idea from an old Peanuts cartoon** in which Snoopy, thinking he is a rhino, goes around head-butting everybody. Sounds silly—well, it *is* I guess—but that's the point! ∽ We always shared a laugh after a friendly rhino butt. (It also turned out to be a great stress and tension reliever!) ∽ This custom blossomed into a host of romantic ideas. First came the cute nicknames, like "Rhinoface," "Super Rhino," and many others that are *much* sillier than those, which I'm just too embarrassed to mention! We began to give each other rhino stuffed animals, rhino stickers, rhino trinkets, rhino tee-shirts—anything we could find. Last Christmas **she even adopted a *real* rhinoceros** in my name! We became the proud adoptive parents of Sammy the Rhino, located somewhere in Africa. ∽ This gift giving has been going on for years now. It has now become a friendly little contest to see who can find and give the best rhino present. Family and friends have even gotten into the act. ∽ Then, in February of 1993 I proposed to Kristine on one knee by the harbor next to the Marriott Longwharf Hotel—where we had walked during our first date. **But where are the rhinos, you ask?** Back in the hotel room. I had the entire room covered with rhino paraphernalia. I'd sneaked to the room earlier in the day and decorated it in rhino fashion. I believe it's possible to make a moonlit stroll on a beach unromantic, and a dinner at McDonald's romantic—depending on your mindset. If we can make those ugly rhinos a romantic staple in our relationship, I think it's possible to make nearly *anything* romantic!

– J.J.R., Massachusetts

101 More Ways

1

Without a doubt the most romantic show on TV: *Mad About You.*

2

Revealed here, for the first time, is the mathematical formula for romance!

$$r = a\,(1\text{-}cosA)$$

Actually, this is the formula for a "cardioid"—a somewhat heart-shaped curve. More precisely, for you romantic nerds out there, a cardioid is "the path of a point on a circle that rolls externally, without slipping, on another equal circle." [I *told* you that I can find romance anywhere!]

3

My current favorite romantic album: *The Sacred Fire,* by Nicholas Gunn.

4

Secret Romantic Idea For Guys Only. [This one is worth *five zillion points* in the Relationship Accounting Department.] Videotape the Superbowl. Take your wife out to dinner during the game. (You'll have the whole place to yourselves. I promise.) Watch the game later that night. (Note: Don't listen to the radio, or accept any phone calls from friends who might tell you the outcome of the game.)

Bonus Section

✦

5

If your partner is a beer lover to rival Norm Peterson . . . send the big lovable lug to Beer Camp. The American Museum of Brewing History and Arts, in Fort Mitchell, Kentucky, runs a three-day Beer Camp. The program includes learning all about beer; brewing it; touring the museum; eating food cooked with beer; and yes, tasting a *lot* of different kinds of beers. The cost is $275 per person. Call 800-426-3841 or 606-341-2800.

6

Some recent romantic movie favorites:

- ❧ *A Walk in the Clouds*
- ❧ *Red Firecracker, Green Firecracker*
- ❧ *Like Water for Chocolate*
- ❧ *Bull Durham*
- ❧ *Four Weddings and a Funeral*
- ❧ *The Bridges of Madison County*
- ❧ *Forget Paris*
- ❧ *Beauty and the Beast*
- ❧ *French Kiss*
- ❧ *While You Were Sleeping*

7

Sexy Shoes is a mail-order source for, well, sexy shoes! They stock low-cost versions of designer pumps, mules, ankle-straps, and metal spikes with three-inch to five-and-a-half-inch heels. Call 517-734-4030, or write to Sexy Shoes, 480 North Second Street, Rogers City, Michigan 49779.

8

"Craig" used to tease his wife, "Tricia," saying she was "pretty as a playmate." She said she was too shy to be a *playmate,* but perhaps she'd be his *pin-up girl.* So Craig began calling her his "Pin-Up Girl." It was just a private little thing until . . . Tricia hired an artist to paint a pin-up portrait of *her,* in the Vargas style from the 1940s. She surprised him with it on his 40th birthday. To say that he was "surprised/pleased/amazed/thrilled is an understatement!"

9

Great relationships need to be both **deep** *and* **wide**. **Deep** qualities include intimacy, security and trust. **Wide** qualities include variety, spontaneity and flexibility. [Which do *you* need to work on?]

10

How about an original, signed photograph of your honey's hero, favorite movie star or celebrity?! ✳ Humphrey Bogart ✳ Judy Garland ✳ George Gershwin ✳ Cole Porter ✳ and over 5,000 more! Call for a free catalog: 908-747-3858. Or write to: Recollections, The Galleria, 2-40 Bridge Avenue #3, Red Bank, New Jersey 07701.

11

Most Romantic Piano Concertos (take my word for it):

- **Mozart's** Piano Concerto No. 21 in C
- **Beethoven's** Piano Concerto No. 5 in E flat
- **Schumann's** Concerto in A Minor for Piano & Orchestra
- **Grieg's** Concerto in A Minor for Piano & Orchestra

12

Think about when and where you use your imagination most effectively and easily: While working? While gardening? While golfing? While caring for kids? Okay . . . now channel that same energy and imagination into your next lovemaking session.

13

Finding Gifts In Everyday Life. A good concept, don't you think? It's also the title of a good book by Nancy Coey. In bookstores or call 919-848-9743.

Bonus Section

14

Sally used to complain that Jack never complimented her. After pondering this, Jack realized, "It's not that I don't love you, or that I don't have nice things to say. It's just that I never think to say them *on my own*." With that insight, he instituted "Dial-A-Compliment" just for her. Sally could call him any time of the day or night and receive a spontaneous and heartfelt compliment!

15

"WHAT WOULD YOU DO WITH CHOCOLATE BODY PAINT?" said the headline in The Celebration Fantastic Catalog. Well, I'm *certainly* not going to tell you *my* answer! But if you want to try it for yourself, you can get a set of "His & Hers" 8 oz. jars—made from semi-sweet French chocolate and heavy cream—for just $15 by calling 800-CELEBRATE.

16

Romantic homework:
Use each of these traits to generate three romantic ideas:

✳ Sense of humor ✳ Childlike wonder ✳ Pure creativity ✳

17

More romantic homework:
Create two romantic gestures that fit each of these descriptions:

❖ Classic and conservative but thoughtful in the extreme
❖ Sexy to the point of nearly being illegal
❖ Totally unexpected from a person of your personality style

18

Life Is More Than Your To-Do List. A great philosophy. Also the title of a great book by Maggie Bedrosian. At bookstores or call 301-460-3408.

1001 plus 101

19

800-72-MUSIC . . . connects you to The Wireless Music Source. You can order virtually any recording currently available in the USA on CD or cassette. Nearly 100,000 titles are available, covering every category of music. Of special interest: They'll help you search for songs. For instance: If all you have is a single song title, they'll find the album it's on. You can also locate recordings by artist, composer, musical genre, instrumentation, and many other attributes.

20

Want to spice-up the presentation of a special meal? Buy a little hunk of dry ice from your local ice house. Put it in a bowl of water, and place it on your serving tray. You'll create wondrous, billowing white clouds!

21

Not that it matters, but I was just thinking . . .

☞ Why do we have birthday cakes and wedding cakes, but no anniversary cakes or Valentine cakes?

☞ Why do we have Christmas tree ornaments, but no special ornaments with which to celebrate other special occasions?

☞ Why is Columbus Day a national holiday, and Valentine's Day isn't?

22

If you're anywhere near San Diego, California in the spring, you *must* visit The Flower Fields at Carlsbad Ranch. Picture a hillside above the Pacific shoreline, with acres and acres and acres of ranunculus plants blooming in ribbon-like bands of color. Admission is free! For more info call 619-930-9123. {Special thanks to W.L.L., California}

Bonus Section

23-25

Recent catalog discoveries!

✦ *For Counsel*—A whole darn catalog full of stuff for lawyers! Who would have thought . . . Call 800-637-0098.

✦ *Old Glory Distributing Co.*—The ultimate rock 'n roll catalog! All kinds of groovy—*way cool!?*—clothing, concert memorabilia and stuff. Call 800-203-8319.

✦ *Tailwinds*—For the pilot or aviation nut! Aviation clothing, authentic flight jackets, jewelry, etc. Call 800-992-7737.

26-28

Recent musical discoveries!

✶ *Forest*—The new CD from our favorite piano man, George Winston.

✶ *MCMXC a.D.*—A pulsing, erotic album by Enigma. With songs like "Principles of Lust" and "Knocking on Forbidden Doors," it's a great accompaniment to lovemaking. [A little irreverent, but . . . sometimes it suits the mood.]

✶ *The Friends of Mr. Cairo*—by Jon (Anderson, of Yes) and Vangelis. Quirky, wonderful music. The song "State of Independence" includes some of the best love verses ever written.

29

If your partner is sensitive about his or her age, but you still want to find some way to celebrate, here's a solution: Count *blessings* instead of years! You could make lists on scrolls of all that the two of you are thankful for. You could focus on a different blessing at each celebration. You could take turns creating the list. You could celebrate several times a year!

1001 plus 101

30

Three romantic albums from Eric Tingstad and Nancy Rumbel. Beautiful, thoughtful, soft music.

🌰 *Homeland* 🌰 *Give and Take* 🌰 *In the Garden*

31

And three romantic albums from Enya. Her ethereal voice will create a romantic mood in any environment.

🎵 *Shepherd Moons* 🎵 *Watermark* 🎵 *The Celts*

32-34

More catalogs for you to peruse.

❋ *The Vermont Teddy Bear Company*—Hand-made Teddy bears. Cool. Call 800-829-2327.

❋ *Past Times*—"Fine Gifts from Great Britain Inspired by the Past." Known by travelers for their 50 stores throughout Britain and Ireland, Past Times now brings its wares to us via catalog. Call 800-621-6020.

❋ *Williams-Sonoma*—"A Catalog for Cooks." Great stuff for your lover's kitchen. Call 800-541-2233.

35-37

And some great musical "samplers" of acoustic/instrumental/New Age music on the Narada label. Each CD contains more than a dozen different artists, all of whom have their own albums.

🌱 *Romance: Music for Piano*
🌱 *The Wilderness Collection*
🌱 *Sampler #1* ❋ And *Sampler #2* ❋ And *Sampler #3*

38

For adults with a playful attitude and a flair for fantasy, The Fantasy Inn in Lake Tahoe has 16 romantic suites, each with a different theme. ☆ *The Romeo and Juliet Suite* ☆ *The Rain Forest Suite* ☆ *The Roman Suite* ☆ *The Marie Antoinette Suite* ☆ *The Graceland/Hollywood Suite* ☆ Each room is designed and decorated down to the last detail to enhance the fantasy environment. Call the Fantasy Inn (for a free brochure with pictures of all the rooms!) in South Lake Tahoe, California, at 800-367-7736 or write to 3696 Lake Tahoe Boulevard, South Lake Tahoe, California 96150.

And . . . they have the most romantic ski package in Lake Tahoe . . . *and,* they offer Romance/Honeymoon packages . . . *and,* they have a full-service wedding chapel and minister on-site.

39

Get your honey tickets to be in the audience of his or her favorite TV show:

✳ For *Saturday Night Live,* call 212-664-3056.
✳ For *Late Night with David Letterman,* call 212-975-2476.
✳ For *Donahue,* call 212-664-4444.

40

You haven't *really* been on a romantic Caribbean vacation until you've experienced one of Sandals Resorts. These folks really, truly know how to create a romantic atmosphere. When they say "Ultra all-inclusive luxury resorts for couples only" they *mean* it! Luxurious accommodations, unbelievable service, no kids, no hassles, no pulling out your wallet every time you turn around. They have several resorts on Jamaica, Antigua, St. Lucia and Barbados. Call Sandals at 800-SANDALS!

41

Is your honey a *Wizard of Oz* fanatic? Well, take her to the Judy Garland Museum! Rare photos, video documentaries, rare recordings and memorabilia. They host a Judy Garland Festival every year, too! The Yellow Brick Road is in Grand Rapids, Minnesota. Call 218-326-6431.

1001 plus 101

42

I've recently discovered a wine company that *really* takes romance seriously. The folks at Blossom Hill produce a range of delicious *and* reasonably priced wines—from Chardonnay to Merlot. They're available wherever fine wine is sold, from well-stocked supermarkets to liquor stores. Blossom Hill understands that the *presentation* is just as important as the *product* (or gift). Thus, each bottle has an elegant label featuring flowers in pinks and purples . . . a nice touch of class that will add to the atmosphere of your romantic encounter. So not only does it *taste* good, but it *looks* good, too!

43

A *must* for your Romantic Music Library: *Sunny*, by rising superstar singer and inspirational speaker Willie Jolley. This recording is a collection of Willie's jazz-style interpretations of classics such as "Ain't No Sunshine" and "My Funny Valentine."

Just $12.99, from InspirTainment Plus. Write to them at 5711 13th Street NW, Suite 100, Washington, D.C. 20011. Or call 202-723-8863.

44

❦ Keep a wedding photo of the two of you on your desk—to remind you of that special day.

❦ Keep a photo of your partner *as a child* in your wallet—to remind you to nurture the tender, special side of him or her.

45

Have you ever wanted to create a life-sized casting of one of your partner's body parts? [Well, *some* people have expressed an interest . . .] Bodyparts Lifecasting is available from Flax Art & Design for just $24. It's a kit that allows you to create a flexible mold, remove it, then fill it with a plaster-like material. You can make rigid or flexible parts. Call 800-547-7778.

Bonus Section *46-48*

Bed & Breakfast Update:

🎵 **New Mexico**—The Don Gaspar Compound, in Santa Fe's historic district, is a classic Mission and Adobe style home. Its six private suites enjoy a secluded adobe-walled garden courtyard. Call 505-986-8664.

🎵 **Maine**—Enjoy turn of the century romantic elegance at the Inn at Long Lake, in Naples. The guest rooms have been restored to their original country warmth with select antique furnishings, fluffy comforters and pillows. Call 800-437-0328 (in Maine, 207-693-6226).

🎵 **Louisiana**—The Terrell House, circa 1858, is an elegant inn located in the Lower Garden District of New Orleans. The house surrounds you with Southern charm, antique chandeliers, marble fireplaces and elegant parlors. It's located on a street of antique shops and jazz clubs.

49

"How to Bed and Breakfast." It has come to my attention that there are some guys out there who, having made reservations at a romantic bed and breakfast, have arrived there and proceeded to turn on the TV. *No, no, no!* Do I have to give you guys minute-by-minute instructions??

Some thoughts:

🎶 Call ahead and make reservations at a recommended local restaurant.

🎶 Set your VCR at home before you leave, so you won't miss your favorite TV shows.

🎶 Enjoy a bubblebath or jacuzzi together.

🎶 Bring some inspiring books to read.

🎶 Do some "Couples Exercises"—like writing down your goals for the next five years; listing the reasons why you love one another. [See my third book, *Romance 101,* for many more exercises.]

🎶 Hide your watches in a drawer—go all weekend without bothering with the time.

🎶 A little "afternoon delight."

🎶 Ask your bed and breakfast hosts for suggestions. They always know their communities very well.

1001 plus 101

50

And here are some specific Bed and Breakfast resource books for you.

~ *Bed & Breakfasts and Country Inns—Inspected, Rated and Approved.* The B&Bs listed here have all been visited personally and rated by the American Bed & Breakfast Association. They have all passed a yearly, on-site, "white glove" inspection. Guaranteed quality!

~ *Bed and Breakfast U.S.A.,* by Betty Rundback. A huge guide, with over 1,200 listings! Includes favorite B&B recipes and a special section for travelers with disabilities.

~ *Recommended Romantic Inns,* from the authors of the Recommended Country Inns Series. Chosen especially for their romantic qualities, these 140 B&Bs are described in detail by the authors, who have visited every site.

51

Shopping for cool/romantic/unusual gifts? If you're near Rochester, New York, you *must* visit The Parkleigh. It's more than a gift shop . . . it's a fun and quirky place, and you never know what you're going to find in there. I re-stock my Gift Closet whenever I visit.

If you're not near Rochester, you can reach The Parkleigh through the Internet! The Parkleigh On-Line Catalog can be reached by calling http;// www.parkleigh.com. The Parkleigh itself is located at 215 Park Avenue, Rochester, New York 14607. Call 'em at 716-244-4842.

52

If luxury and adventure are your goals, you might want to consider taking your lover on one of these outrageous/deluxe vacations created by INTRAV:

⊛ A voyage to the North Pole, aboard a Russian nuclear icebreaker.
⊛ Celebrate Christmas on safari in Kenya.

For more info, call the masters of luxury holidays at INTRAV at 800-456-8100. Or write to 7711 Bonhomme Avenue, St. Louis, Missouri 63105.

53

Everyone knows that diamonds are the ultimate expression of love—but *not* everyone knows how to go about selecting and buying a quality diamond. So here's a brief-but-complete two-part lesson for you:

♦ **Become educated:** The book *How to Buy a Diamond,* by Fred Cuellar, is the #1 bestseller on diamonds. It's easy to read and surprisingly detailed. This book is a *must* for you if you're about to become engaged. It's also the best resource for *anyone* who's in the market for diamonds. Available in bookstores or by calling 800-275-4047. ♦ ♦ ♦ ♦ ♦ ♦

♦ **Find a *great* jeweler:** After years of keeping this to myself, I'm going to share with you my personal jeweler. Fred Cuellar (see above!) knows more about diamonds than I know about romance! He's ranked among the top 20 experts in America by the Jewelers Board of Trade; he has a handpicked staff of experts; and he helps people save hundreds—or thousands!—of dollars on their diamonds. Fred is not your average jeweler: He created "the world's most expensive toy"—a 185-carat jeweled Rubik's Cube! And he created a million-dollar hockey puck for the Houston Aeros! Cool, huh?! ♦ ♦ ♦ ♦ ♦ ♦ ♦ ♦ ♦ ♦ ♦ ♦ ♦ ♦

You can reach Diamond Cutters International by calling 800-275-4047 or 713-22CARAT, or by writing to them at 4265 San Felipe, Suite 960, Houston, Texas 77027. ♦ ♦ ♦ ♦ ♦ ♦ ♦ ♦ ♦ ♦ ♦ ♦ ♦

54

What do *you* do with old greeting cards from your honey? You don't just toss them away, do you?! *Heaven forbid!* True romantics . . .

❧ Display them on mantles and tables.
❧ Set them on their desks at work.
❧ Have them mounted and framed.
❧ Put them in a scrapbook.
❧ Toss 'em in a file—to use in some creative way in the future.
❧ Paste 'em on a collage.
❧ And one crazy couple in my Romance Class actually *wallpapered an entire room in their house with greeting cards!*

1001 plus 101

55-57

You *could* also visit . . .

❋ *The World of Coca-Cola*—a museum of Coca-Cola history. More Coke memorabilia than you thought possible! Vintage TV commercials, the first Coke can in space, etc. Located at 55 Martin Luther King Jr. Drive, Atlanta, Georgia 30303. Call 404-676-5151.

❋ *Tupperware's Museum of Historic Food Containers*—featuring the ancestors of Tupperware, beginning with an Egyptian bowl dated 2500 B.C. Located just 20 minutes from Disney World, at 3175 North Orange Blossom Trail, Kissimmee, Florida 34744. Or call 800-858-7221.

❋ There's even a *guidebook* for all sorts of factory tours: *Watch It Made in the U.S.A.,* by Bruce Brumberg & Karen Axelrod.

58

Custom jigsaw puzzles to challenge your puzzle lover! High quality, custom work is priced at about $1.50 per square inch, by the folks at J.C. Ayer & Co. Call 'em at 508-741-1522.

59

Get a little bottle. (Maybe an antique bottle. Maybe an old spice bottle. Something cool.) Fill it with sand. Cork it. Label it: "Extra Time." Give it to your partner. [Inspired by Jim Croce's song "Time In A Bottle."]

60

✦ **The note:** "Let's go sparkin' in the dark"—attached to . . .
✦ **The item:** A roll of Wint-O-Green Lifesavers.
✦ **The effect:** They "spark" slightly when you bite down own them while in the dark.
✦ **Also:** Pep-O-Mint Lifesavers work, too.

Bonus Section

61

Songs to help you express your feelings. **Friendship & Appreciation** . . .

- ♦♦ *That's What Friends Are For,* Dionne Warwick
- ♦♦ *Bridge Over Troubled Waters,* Simon & Garfunkel
- ♦♦ *Thank You For Being A Friend,* Andrew Gold
- ♦♦ *You've Got A Friend,* James Taylor (and Carole King, too)
- ♦♦ *Stand By Me,* Ben E. King

62

Songs to help you express your feelings. **Desire & Sexual Attraction** . . .

- ➤ *Sexual Healing,* Marvin Gaye
- ➤ *I Feel Like Makin' Love,* Bad Company
- ➤ *I Want Your Sex,* George Michael
- ➤ *Afternoon Delight,* Starland Vocal Band
- ➤ *Let's Spend The Night Together,* Rolling Stones
- ➤ *Natural Woman,* Aretha Franklin

63

Songs to help you express your feelings. **Loneliness & Missing You** . . .

- ☞ *Wishing You Were Here,* Chicago
- ☞ *Far Away,* Carole King
- ☞ *Missing You,* Jim Reeves
- ☞ *I Miss You Like Crazy,* Natalie Cole
- ☞ *Missing You Now,* Michael Bolton

64

Songs to help you express your feelings. **Anniversary & Celebrations** . . .

- ♥ *Always And Forever,* Heatwave
- ♥ *Forever And Ever, Amen,* Randy Travis
- ♥ *Our Love Is Here To Stay,* Harry Connick, Jr.
- ♥ *The Anniversary Song,* Richard Tucker
- ♥ *More Today Than Yesterday,* Spiral Staircase

1001 plus 101

65

Songs to help you express your feelings. **Love/Tender. . .**

- ❤ *Lady,* Kenny Rogers
- ❤ *Endless Love,* Diana Ross
- ❤ *Always On My Mind,* Willie Nelson
- ❤ *Just The Way You Are,* Billy Joel
- ❤ *I Honestly Love You,* Olivia Newton John
- ❤ *You Are So Beautiful (To Me),* Joe Cocker
- ❤ *Through The Years,* Kenny Rogers
- ❤ *Longer Than,* Dan Fogelberg
- ❤ *Evergreen,* Barbra Streisand

66

Songs to help you express your feelings. **Love/Intense . . .**

- ❣ *When A Man Loves A Woman,* Percy Sledge
- ❣ *Crazy For You,* Madonna
- ❣ *Wind Beneath My Wings,* Bette Midler
- ❣ *Closer To Believing,* Emerson, Lake & Palmer
- ❣ *I Am Waiting,* Yes
- ❣ *I Will Always Love You,* Whitney Houston
- ❣ *Nights In White Satin,* Moody Blues

67

Songs to help you express your feelings. **Love/Joy . . .**

- 🎵 *Love Me Do,* Beatles
- 🎵 *I Just Called To Say I Love You,* Stevie Wonder
- 🎵 *You Are The Sunshine Of My Life,* Stevie Wonder
- 🎵 *The Way You Do The Things You Do,* Temptations
- 🎵 *What A Wonderful World,* Louis Armstrong
- 🎵 *How Sweet It Is,* James Taylor
- 🎵 *It Had To Be You,* Harry Connick, Jr.

68-69

If you believe that the way to your man's heart is through his stomach, send gourmet!

✤ "Orange-red HoneyBell oranges"—considered by some to be the sweetest, juiciest, most flavorful oranges anywhere. From the Cushman Fruit Company. Call 800-776-7575, or write 3325 Forest Hill Boulevard, West Palm Beach, Florida 33406.

✤ Winner of the coveted New York Magazine "Best Cheese Cake in New York" award: The "World's Finest" cheesecake from Junior's Restaurant. Call 800-958-6467 or 718-852-5257, or visit them at 386 Flatbush Avenue Extension, Brooklyn, New York 11201.

70

Your physical surroundings affect your emotional well-being. While many of us would agree with this, the Chinese art of *feng shui* takes it to quite another level. Feng shui regards homes, buildings and rooms as "energy systems" that affect *qi*—our basic life energy. It makes sense to me that we should do everything possible to create personal environments that support our lives and our loves. Here are two books to help you learn more: *Feng Shui: Art and Harmony of Place,* by Johndennis Govert. *Interior Design With Feng Shui,* by Sarah Rossbach.

71

If I suggested that you vacation in world-famous romantic Winterset, Iowa, you'd probably think I was kidding . . . until I told you that Winterset is located in Madison County—an area known for its *bridges.* You can visit the bridges of Madison County any time—but you may want to plan a trip in October, when the town sponsors an annual Covered Bridge Festival (which was going on for *decades* before the publication of *The Bridges of Madison County.)* For more info, call 800-298-6119.

1001 plus 101

72

Little Rules of Love

* *Share something.* A cup of tea. A glass of wine. A bubblebath. A good joke. An extra 10 minutes in bed in the morning.
* *Save your partner one minute.* Wipe the snow from her windshield. Open the newspaper to his favorite section. Get up a few minutes early to start the coffee.
* *Pamper each other.* Give him a foot massage. Prepare her favorite meal. Do his least favorite chore for him. Act-out her favorite fantasy.
* *Make a deal.* "I'll do this for you, if you'll do that for me"—may not sound romantic, but it can get the romantic ball rolling!

73

Consider the telephone. For some it is their *favorite* medium of romance. Now, before you hang up on this concept, consider . . . ☎ The sound of your lover's voice on the phone. ☎ The sweet agony of waiting for him to call. ☎ "Hi. It's me."—And knowing who Me is. ☎ The familiar pattern of the tones made by your lover's telephone number. ☎ Calling to leave a favorite song on the answering machine. No message, just music. ☎

74

Have you noticed how many people are flying custom-made flags in front of their homes? Most of them are celebrating major holidays or seasons. But *some* of them are secret messages to their partners. Here are a few ideas from my Romance Class participants:

☆ **Hearts** = "I'm in a romantic mood."
☆ **Skull and crossbones** = "Watch out—I've had a bad day."
☆ **Candles** = "No food in the house. Let's eat dinner out."
☆ **Fireworks** = "Let's make love tonight."
☆ **Exclamation point** = "The kids are driving me bonkers!"

Bonus Section

75

A *Daily* Romantic Checklist

❏ Compliment your partner.
❏ Spend 20 minutes of uninterrupted time together.
❏ Check-in with each other during the day.
❏ Perform one small—and *unexpected*—gesture.
❏ Say "I love you" at least three times.
❏ Thank your partner for something.
❏ Look for romantic concepts in the newspaper.
❏ Take an extra minute when kissing good-bye.

76

A *Weekly* Romantic Checklist

❏ Bring home one small, unexpected gift or present.
❏ Share some form of physical intimacy.
❏ Share an entire afternoon or evening together.
❏ Share two insights you gained this week.
❏ Write at least one little love note.
❏ Mail something to your partner.
❏ Plan something special for the upcoming weekend.

77

A *Monthly* Romantic Checklist

❏ Plan one romantic surprise for this month.
❏ Re-stock your stash of greeting cards.
❏ Go out to dinner once or twice.
❏ Rent at least two romantic movies.
❏ Make love!
❏ Make plans for a three-day romantic weekend sometime in the next three months.
❏ Plan one romantic event with a seasonal theme.

1001 plus 101

78

A *Yearly* Romantic Checklist

❏ Make a New Year's resolution to be a more creative romantic.
❏ Make plans for your next anniversary.
❏ Think of an unusual way to celebrate your partner's birthday.
❏ Review your plans for your next vacation.
❏ Create a special "Romance" category in your household budget.
❏ Make plans for Valentine's Day—well in advance!

79

You say you need **more time** in order to be more romantic? So *create more time!* The strategies on how to do so are in a great little book called *How To Put Ten Hours In An Eight Hour Day,* by Kay Johnson. Check the business section of a bookstore or call 800-444-2524.

80

My friends Jack Canfield and Mark Victor Hansen have both devoted their lives to helping and inspiring others through their seminars and speeches. They recently collected *thousands* of *awesome,* inspirational stories, and sorted through them to choose the best-of-the-best to share with you in their wonderful books *Chicken Soup for the Soul* and *A 2nd Helping of Chicken Soup for the Soul.* These life-affirming stories will warm your heart and inspire your love of life. If your local bookstore is out of stock, call 800-441-5569 to order copies. [Be on the look-out for several more inspiring books from these guys in the next few years.]

81

LoveNotes ✷ *"Listening is an act of love."* ✷ *"The balance between closeness and separateness must be respected."* ✷ From Larry James' second book, *LoveNotes For Lovers.* His first is *How To Really Love The One You're With.* In bookstores and by calling 800-725-9223.

Bonus Section

82

Don't you just *love* these book titles? ✦ *Profound Stuff* ✦ *Stuff That Works Every Single Day* ✦ *101 Things That Make You Say UNGAWA!* ✦ They're from author/speaker Larry Winget, who is an expert in motivation and success strategies. His books are humorous, flamboyant, practical and easy-to-read. His ideas transcend typical business philosophy and go beyond the clichés of most self-help teachings. Look for them in your local bookstore or call 800-749-4597.

83

Beware of the "passive pull" of television. It can suck up massive amounts of time that could otherwise be spent actively enjoying life with your lover. From the book *Unplugging the Plug-In Drug*, by Marie Winn: "Television's attraction is so powerful precisely because it gratifies that passive side of human nature that all of us, adults and children, are endowed with in different degrees. Consequently, an important step toward a more active and satisfying family life is to become aware of this passive pull, to assess its power, and to consciously struggle against it."

84

Act Now! Good idea. Also a good book. Sub-titled "Successful Acting Techniques You Can Use Everyday to Dramatically Improve Health, Wealth, and Relationships," this book is a treasure, from Dale L. Anderson, M.D., and experienced doctor with a variety of interests, who is leading the way in combining traditional medicine with alternative methods. In bookstores or call 800-848-2793.

85

Try this . . . Kiss the open palm of your lover's hand. Then roll-up her fingers, making a fist. Then say, "Save this in case of emergencies." {Thanks to M.S.D., New York}

1001 plus 101

86

Since we all have a unique set of talents, abilities, aptitudes and desires, our "styles of romance" differ. Therefore, a key to being more romantic is to understand yourself better. *Rethinking Yourself—Finding Your Natural Path For Growth* is a fabulous, self-contained, six-cassette learning system from Jim Cathcart that will help you understand yourself, your motivations and your strengths better. You'll learn the power of The Acorn Principle: "Your greatest, fastest and easiest growth always comes from your natural abilities." Call 800-222-4883 or 619-558-8855, or write to Post Office Box 9075, La Jolla, California 92038.

87

Romantics can sometimes run into legal troubles. ✗ In Halethorpe, Maryland, it is against the law to kiss for more than one minute. ✗ In Springfield, Massachusetts, cab drivers are forbidden from making love in the front seats of their taxis while working. ✗ In Connecticut, a man may not write love letters to a woman whose mother has forbidden him from seeing her. (From *The Trenton Pickle Ordinance and Other Cockeyed Americana,* by D. Hyman.)

88

Do you value productivity, accomplishment and efficiency? But do you *also* value peace, serenity and repose? "Our constant activity leaves us little time for intimacy or reflection, for an appreciation of nature or the joy of simply being present," says one of my favorite authors, Linda Weltner. In lamenting the loss of Sunday as a day of rest in our busy culture, she writes, "In a culture where making money is a primary goal and spending it our chief satisfaction, what can you say in favor of ensuring leisure time for families and individuals?"

Some of Linda Weltner's finest columns have been collected in a book called *No Place Like Home.* It's a wonderful, warm book. Not yet available in bookstores—but you can order a copy *directly* by calling 617-631-7501.

Bonus Section

89

Jealousy has two sources: 1) Lack of maturity, and/or 2) Lack of self-esteem. If you're troubled by jealousy, you need to work on *yourself,* not on your partner. The cornerstone of solid relationships is trust. The next foundation pieces are trust and honesty.

90

Romantic background music? Glad you asked. Here are some of my readers' favorite recording artists:

✦ Tom Scott	✦ Harry Connick, Jr.	✦ Yanni
✦ George Benson	✦ George Winston	✦ Enya
✦ Natalie Cole	✦ Billie Holiday	✦ David Sanborn
✦ Kenny G	✦ Stan Getz	✦ Earl Klugh
✦ David Lanz	✦ Andreas Vollenweider	✦ Liz Story
✦ William Ackerman	✦ Grover Washington, Jr.	✦ Luther Vandross
✦ David Benoit	✦ Richard Clayderman	✦ Larry Carlton

91

For your guy: How about a set of 12 boxer shorts—one for each month—with seasonally themed patterns on them. Red hearts for February. Shamrocks for March. Baseballs for May. Stars & stripes for July. Etc.! Just $16 per pair. Call The Celebration Fantastic catalog at 800-CELEBRATE.

92

A night on the town ∞ A lazy afternoon in a hammock ∞ A day without the kids ∞ A morning lounging in bed ∞ A breakfast without newspapers ∞ A walk on a beach ∞ A picnic in the park ∞ A recording of "Your Song" ∞ An evening of dancing ∞ A three-day weekend ∞ A kiss on the cheek ∞ A bottle of champagne ∞ An intimate conversation ∞ A surprise vacation ∞ A secret pet name.

1001 *plus* 101

93

Down comforters ❧ Feather beds ❧ Extra pillows

94

Her husband was a handyman. Loved to take things apart and put them back together again. She gave him a fancy VCR for his birthday . . . took it apart and gave it to him wrapped in 16 different boxes!

95

She gave him a note, written on poster paper—included were 13 candy bars glued in the appropriate places. It read:

Dear **Hot Tamales,**
    I thought about taking you to the **Symphony** or giving you **100 Grand,** but **Mr. Goodbar** said no, you deserve more.
    Your little **Runts** said their **Sugar Daddy** needs **Extra Bit-O-Honey!**
    So this weekend while our **Sugar Babies** are gone, let's **Snickers Good and Plenty** in Oklahoma City.

Hugs & **Kisses,**
Your **Kit Kat**

{Thanks to K.E.S., Oklahoma}

96

She loved "shoe string licorice." He wrote her a message in licorice letters one day: "*Love ya, babe.*" She ate it up!

Bonus Section

97

During their seven years of dating he'd given her many flowers. During their long-awaited wedding ceremony she surprised him with a room-full of flowers—the very flowers he had given her. She'd had every flower he'd ever given her carefully and lovingly dried or pressed.

98

She received a gift for no special occasion. A beautifully wrapped box from Tiffany's! She opened it to find a sterling silver tray—engraved with "Sally, will you marry me?"

99

She hung a 36-inch-wide strip of butcher paper on the wall. She then painted her body with water based red tempera paint, then struck a pose and pressed her painted body against the paper—creating a very personalized and definitely one-of-a-kind work of art. She let it dry, rolled it up, tied it with a red ribbon, and gave it to her husband for Valentine's Day. He still talks about it to this day.

100

He always did have a tendency to "overdo" things. One year he rented a limousine for her birthday. She enjoyed it so much that the following year he rented the limo *again* . . . but this time he rented it *for an entire week!* So in addition to their fancy night on the town, she got chauffeured to the super market, to the dry cleaner, to church; the kids got chauffeured to school, to soccer practice, to the playground. A memorable experience for one and all!

1001 plus 101

101

Do you know the difference between the "urgent" and the "important"?

✦ The **urgent** is what demands your attention *right now:* Deadlines, details and short-term priorities. It *may* be what's important to you, but more often it reflects the priorities of *others.*

✦ The **important** is what reflects *your* priorities and values. It is more long-term in nature *and therefore easier to defer.*

Love is **important**—car troubles are **urgent**. Beware of the urgent eclipsing the important in your life!

❧

*The history of humankind is
the story of our search for love.*

~ GJPG

An Invitation

These books and seminars are part of the Grand Conversation, as Greg calls it. He sees his books as "The beginning of a *dialogue*, and not merely another long-winded *monologue* by some so-called 'expert'." Our readers are an integral part of that dialogue. We'd love to hear from you! ∼ You are invited to write to us with your romantic ideas and your romantic stories—whether sentimental, outrageous or creative. They may end up in the *LoveLetter Newsletter*, or perhaps in a future book. We will credit you by name or protect your anonymity, as you wish. —Or just write to say *Hi!*

Gregory J.P. Godek
Casablanca Press, Inc.
P.O. Box 226
Weymouth, Massachusetts 02188-0001

Romance Seminars

Greg presents keynote speeches and seminars for a variety of organizations nationally and internationally. ∼ Greg's *speeches* range from 30-minute motivational talks to hour-long inspirational keynote lectures. Every presentation is custom-tailored to the audience he is addressing. Greg's *seminars* range from 2-hour sessions to day-long workshops, depending on the organization's needs. The seminars are high-energy, interactive sessions that are designed specifically for each different situation. For more info, please write to the address above or call: 617-340-1300.

Romance Across America 1996-'97

Gregory J.P. Godek's 50-State/150-City/21-Month Book Tour

Greg will be bringing his Romance Seminar to all of America in 1996 and 1997. He and his wife, Tracey, will be touring the country in their 36-foot Holiday Rambler RV {"Romance Vehicle"}. They invite you to participate in a seminar, enjoy a once-in-a-lifetime experience, and make an investment in your relationship. For regular updates on the "Romance Across America" tour, send your name and address to: LoveLetter, P.O. Box 226, Weymouth MA 02188. Or call 800-LOVE-026.

Tour highlights

∾ The trip will cover all 50 states.
∾ Romance Seminars will be held in 150 cities.
∾ 96% of the U.S. population will be within 100 miles of Godek's events.
∾ Total trip mileage is 21,037 miles.
∾ The trip will be conducted over 21 months— February 1996 through October 1997.
∾ Booksignings will be held in 500 bookstores— that's 10% of all the bookstores in America.

Romance Coupon

1001 Ways To Be Romantic

∿

This coupon entitles the holder to one candlelit dinner . . .
(with the issuer of the coupon)—
at the most romantic restaurant in town!

∿

A gift to _____

A gift from _____

Romance Coupon

1001 Ways To Be Romantic

∿

This coupon entitles the holder to one Weekend Get-Away!
Here's the deal: The coupon holder gets to choose the weekend,
and the coupon issuer gets to choose the location.

∿

A gift to _____

A gift from _____

Romance Coupon

1001 Ways To Be Romantic

Nightgowns! Teddies!! Stockings!!! Garter belts!!!!
This coupon is good for a $100 shopping spree
in the nearest lingerie store or lingerie catalog.

A gift to _____

A gift from _____

Romance Coupon

1001 Ways To Be Romantic

This coupon entitles the holder to—*flowers!*
Your choice: One dozen of any one kind of flower.
Flowers to be delivered within three days of issuance of coupon.

A gift to _____

A gift from _____

Romance Coupon

1001 Ways To Be Romantic

∼

This coupon entitles the holder to one luxurious bubblebath . . .
complete with champagne & candles.
P L U S
Bonus! One sensual toweling off.

∼

A gift to _____

A gift from _____

Romance Coupon

1001 Ways To Be Romantic

∼

This coupon entitles the holder to one *sensuous* backrub,
performed by the issuer of the coupon.
Time limit: No less than 30 minutes in duration!

∼

A gift to _____

A gift from _____

Romance Coupon

1001 Ways To Be Romantic

~

This coupon entitles the holder to **3** full hours of uninterrupted peace and quiet. The coupon holder gets to choose the time. The coupon issuer is responsible for the removal of all distractions.

~

A gift to _____

A gift from _____

Romance Coupon

1001 Ways To Be Romantic

~

Breakfast In Bed.

~

A gift to _____

A gift from _____

Romance Coupon

1001 Ways To Be Romantic

∞

This is a "Romantic ABCs Coupon."
The coupon holder chooses one letter of the alphabet.
The coupon issuer will create a day of romance
with gifts and gestures that all begin with that letter.

∞

A gift to _____

A gift from _____

Romance Coupon

1001 Ways To Be Romantic

∽

_____

_____

_____

∽

A gift to _____

A gift from _____

✦ INDEX ✦

V

W

X

Y

Z

Order Form

—— *Books* ——

✦ *1001 Ways To Be Romantic*—335 pages, 5-1/2" x 8-1/2"...................$14.95
✦ *1001 More Ways To Be Romantic*—307 pages, 5-1/2" x 8-1/2"........$11.95
✦ *Romance 101*—269 pages, 5-1/2" x 8-1/2"..$12.95
✦ *The Portable Romantic*—139 pages, 4-1/2" x 6"...................................$6.95
✦ *The Lovers' Bedside Companion*—143 pages, 4-1/2" x 6"....................$6.95
✦ *Loving: A Journal of Our Relationship*—160 pages, 6" x 6"..............$7.95

Call Toll-Free
800-LOVE-026

Major credit cards accepted. Shipping charges vary with quantities ordered
and method of delivery.

—— *Newsletter* ——

❖ A free one-year subscription to *the newsletter of romantic ideas*—
the *LoveLetter*—is now available for the asking. It's a $25 value, and
it's full of creative, unusual and wonderful ideas, gifts and gestures.

❖ Sign-up yourself, your spouse, your boyfriend/girlfriend, your
parents, your friends—anyone who needs a good swift kick-in-the-
pants, or would simply appreciate receiving lots of great romantic
ideas on a regular basis.

❖ Send your name & address to: *LoveLetter*, P.O. Box 226, Weymouth,
Massachusetts 02188-0001.

—— *Romance Seminars* ——

☞ You are invited to attend one of Greg's Romance Seminars. He will
be presenting in all 50 states, in 150 cities, during 1996 and 1997.

☞ For details on Greg's "Romance Across America" tour—dates and
times, cities and locations—send for your free subscription to the
LoveLetter Newsletter (see above), which will contain regular updates.